MW01174193

Jeff Graham & Mike Matyjewicz

Edited by Elena Galey-Pride
Cover Photo by Quinton Cruickshanks

Copyright © Sparkling Winos, 2022
Primary photography by Sparkling Winos
Supplementary photography by DepositPhotos

First Edition, April 2022
Made in Canada

ISBN 978-1-7781144-0-3 (Paperback)
ISBN 978-1-7781144-1-0 (Hardcover)
ISBN 978-1-7781144-2-7 (eBook)

sparklingwinos.com
@sparklingwinos

"Jeff and Mike offer up a delicious dive into sparkling wines. This book will inspire you to pop a bottle and explore wine through the world's best bubbles."

– Madeline Puckette, Wine Folly

 **WINE FOLLY**

PART ONE

Sparkling Wine 101

Class is in session! The first half of this book will lay the foundation for you to learn all about sparkling wine and become a sparkling wino yourself.

PART TWO

Our Effervescent Adventures

Join us on a journey around the globe as we take a deeper dive into the world's key sparkling wine producing regions, and share stories and photos from our adventures along the way.

Introduction:

SPARKLING WINE 101

In This Section:

"Sparkling wine can, and should, be enjoyed any day or time of year – certainly not only on special occasions!

What is Sparkling Wine?

In the simplest of definitions, **sparkling wine is a wine that contains carbon dioxide (CO_2)**, which produces those tiny, tingly, delightful bubbles that we all know and love. Yay bubbles! Of course, the science is much more complicated than that, but fear not, **we promise to make learning all about sparkling wine just as easy and enjoyable as tasting it**. After all, bubbly is the most uplifting, festive and fun wine style out there – and learning about it should be too!

What You'll Learn from This Book

You'll find your sparkle. The main goal of this book is to teach you all about the wonderful world of sparkling wine and to arm you with everything you need to know to select the perfect bottle of bubbly for any palate, pairing or occasion. In Chapter 1, we're going to scratch the surface with an overview of the **sparkling spectrum** and, throughout this book, we'll take you on an effervescent adventure, adding a new sparkling skill to your theoretical wine tool belt with each subsequent chapter.

You'll learn how to read and decipher a sparkling wine label. "Wine speak" can be overwhelming, but it certainly doesn't have to be. If you've ever picked up a bottle of bubbly and flipped to the back label to find words such as *tirage*, *lees*, and *terroir* and felt totally lost – we're here for you! In Chapter 2, we'll lay down the foundation for this effervescent wine adventure with our handy sparkling wine glossary. This will arm you with definitions of all the words you'll need to know throughout this book, and it will serve as a helpful guide that you can return to in order to decipher any wine label like a pro. When new terms are introduced, they will appear in italics in the text and the corresponding definition can be found in Chapter 2.

You'll learn how to properly (and safely) open a bottle of sparkling wine. If we had a dollar for every time someone anxiously handed us a bottle of bubbly at a social engagement because they were terrified to open it, we could be enjoying expensive *Champagne* every day! But in all seriousness, many people get nervous when it comes time to pop open a bottle of bubbly. And they should, as there's a ton of pressure contained inside that glass bottle. But trust us, it doesn't have to be scary. In Chapter 3, we'll teach you how to correctly (and safely) open a bottle of sparkling wine. But we won't stop there. We'll also teach you the art of *Sabrage* – opening a bottle of bubbly with a sword – because, let's face it, it's an epic party trick!

You'll learn how to correctly serve, taste, and evaluate sparkling wine. Most times, you've likely served or enjoyed your bubbles in a *flute*, right? Would we blow your mind if we told you that a flute might not be the best glass for bubbly appreciation? In Chapter 4, we'll settle the "Great Glassware Debate" once and for all. We'll share our tips and tricks on properly serving, tasting, and evaluating sparkling wine. While it may seem strange for us to tell you how to taste something, it's with good cause: when you learn to think critically about what's in your glass, you will begin to build a wine library in your brain, and you'll take a massive leap forward on your wine journey. After all, it's all about you!

You'll learn how to pair sparkling wine with food, effortlessly. This book is packed with what we like to call "fizz facts," and guess what our favourite fizz fact is? Sparkling wine is a sommelier's secret weapon. That's right! Most dinner party hosts may ask you, "red or white?" But it's a well-known fact among bubbleheads that sparkling wine is, hands down, the most food-friendly wine style. It pairs perfectly with pretty much everything, and when in doubt, we say, pop the bubbly! In Chapter 5, we'll share our favourite sparkling wine and food pairings – from fool-proof classics to our unconventional go-to's (trust us, you haven't lived until you've had a glass of Champagne with chicken nuggets).

You'll learn how to craft mind-blowing sparkling wine cocktails. Not only does sparkling wine pair flawlessly with food, but it also makes an excellent match with … other adult beverages. Are you looking to up your cocktail game? Just add bubbles! In Chapter 6, we'll share our favourite "Mimosa Hack" and secret sparkling cocktail recipes that will impress your guests and add a little extra sparkle to your next bubbly brunch or celebration.

You'll learn how the grapes are grown for sparkling wine and the main methods used to craft it. To fully understand what something is and how it works, we must first know how it's made. It takes so much work to get that hypnotizing stream of bubbles into the glass in front of you. Once you grasp how different styles of sparkling wine are crafted (and what to expect from them), navigating those wine shop shelves to find the perfect bottle of bubbly will be a breeze. In Chapter 7, we'll take you on a journey from grape to glass, discussing sparkling wine viticulture and winemaking practices so you can better understand and fully appreciate the sparkling wine spectrum!

You'll learn all about the key sparkling wine regions and styles worldwide. Finally, pack your bags and a bottle of bubbly because beginning with Chapter 8, we're taking off on an effervescent trip around the globe! We'll take you through all of our favourite sparkling wine regions, and we'll break down the key sparkling wine styles from each. We'll share some of our favourite photos and memories from our travels, and hopefully, we'll inspire you to venture out and return home with a few new bottles of bubbly to try yourself.

Again, the goal of this book is to help you find your sparkle. Sparkling wine is one of the fastest-growing wine categories around the world. It's fun, festive, and fabulous – and it's a proven mood elevator! It can, and should, be enjoyed any day or time of year – certainly not just on special occasions. We hope to open your mind to the expansive world of sparkling wine and to teach you a new thing or two about this explosive wine style. We'll arm you with everything you need to get the best bubbles for your buck. You'll learn to pair sparkling wine and food effortlessly. And hopefully, we'll help you discover a new style of sparkling wine that appeals to you. So, let's pop a cork and get to it!

Who Are the Sparkling Winos?

Now that you know what to expect from this book, allow us to properly introduce ourselves: **we're Jeff and Mike, but most people just call us the Sparkling Winos**. And as the name would suggest, our affinity for bubbles is unparalleled.

We met each other way back in 2004, and even back then, sparkling wine was always our beverage of choice. At the time, people thought that was rather strange. Every time we ordered a bottle of bubbles at a restaurant, we'd get asked, "what are you celebrating?" "It's Tuesday," we'd say. The server would look at us completely perplexed. Thankfully, sparkling wine outside of a celebratory context has become much more common nowadays. However, there is still a long way to go in solidifying its spot at the dinner table, alongside mainstays such as red and white wine.

As time went on, our interest in sparkling wine continued to blossom, and it grew from a casual curiosity into something more formal. Jeff began with part-time wine studies at George Brown College in Toronto. Later, he completed the Wine & Spirit Education Trust (WSET) program, achieving a Level 3 Award in Wines, with distinction. Our stack of wine books is taller than the two of us, and we're always poking our noses into one or another to see how sparkling wine is presented, only to find that there hasn't been one written how we would write it. And so, here we are!

But we are getting ahead of ourselves.

After the formal wine studies, we quickly became known, at least within our social circle, as "the wine guys." All our vacation time was spent travelling to new wine regions across the globe and, as our interest and knowledge in wine kept expanding, we found ourselves being asked for our opinions and our wine recommendations – well, from our friends, at least! "You should start a blog," they said. We thought long and hard about it and realized that there was indeed a bit of a void in the market. No one with our perspective was focused solely on sparkling wine as a category. Since it was such a staple in our lives and came so naturally to us, we decided we could be that voice, so on October 26, 2016, "Sparkling Winos" was born.

This was around the time that the "influencer" space was picking up steam on social media (truth be told, we both loathe that term). We began to garner much attention for our dynamic and light-hearted approach to sharing our wine knowledge on social media, which we built up to complement and support our blog. Within a few months, we had garnered thousands of followers that quickly grew into tens of thousands of followers. We soon realized that we weren't the only ones under the sparkling wine spell.

Since then, we've hosted countless events and educational seminars, judged wine competitions worldwide, and travelled to nearly every key sparkling wine-producing region. We've even won awards, including VQA Promoter of the Year in 2019, for shining a spotlight on Ontario wine – and we have to say, this remains one of our greatest honours. We've spread the sparkling word on a global stage. Our little passion project became our wildest – and bubbliest – dream come true!

We don't believe that anyone should label themselves an "expert" in any field, as there is always something more to learn, but we certainly have been living, breathing, and sipping all things sparkling wine for a long time, so we sure know our bubbles. And we couldn't be more excited to continue spreading the sparkling love and to share all of our knowledge about this fascinating wine style in a fun, colourful and unpretentious way through this book. Because, as we always say, "When you've got bubbles, you've got no troubles!"

> Our little passion project became our wildest – and bubbliest – dream come true!

Chapter 1:

THE SPARKLING SPECTRUM

In This Section:

The Sparkling Spectrum

There's so much to explore and taste within the exciting and diverse world of sparkling wine – we call it the "sparkling spectrum." We're here to help you navigate the sparkling spectrum and "**find your sparkle**." What does that mean exactly? Well, we hope to open your eyes to the many different styles of sparkling wine, help you find a favourite (or several), and teach you everything you need to know to select the perfect bottle of bubbly for any palate, pairing or occasion.

Sparkling wine is a wine style unto its own, and one expression – whether it be Champagne, *Prosecco* or something else – does not define the entire category. In the past, you've probably heard all sparkling wine referred to as Champagne. You may have even done it yourself. No judgement! We've all been there at some point. But it's important to note that the sparkling spectrum is broad and encompasses many different styles. **While all Champagne is sparkling wine, not all sparkling wine is Champagne**. Champagne only comes from a small region in northern France, just like Prosecco only comes from northeastern Italy, *Cava* from northeastern Spain, etc. You get the idea!

Grouping all sparkling wine together makes as little sense as grouping other major categories of wine, like red or white, under one label or as one expression. You would never group all red and white wines and classify them as the same, right? A crisp New Zealand Sauvignon Blanc is night and day from a rich, buttery California Chardonnay. A bold, brambly Argentine Malbec is a world away from an elegant, lighter-bodied Burgundian Pinot Noir. In these categories, the distinctions may seem more obvious. We think this has to do with the fact that most people are aware of at least some different red or white wine styles and have explored the diversity of these styles of wine through their wine journeys.

Just like red or white wine, sparkling wine is a spectrum too. There are many different grape varieties used to craft sparkling wine. When you consider the different grape varieties grown to produce it, along with the grape's place of origin and the various winemaking techniques and production methods, the opportunities for exploring the sparkling spectrum look endless. But fear not, we are here to guide you through it and to help you find your sparkle!

There are many different ways to make sparkling wine, but, to keep things straightforward in this book, we are going to focus primarily on the two most popular production methods used around the world: the *Traditional Method* (how Champagne is made in France, for example) and the *Charmat Method* (how Prosecco is made in Italy, for one). Neither of these production methods is necessarily "better" than the other. Still, they are quite different and result in two different styles of sparkling wine. Both ways include a **secondary *fermentation*** that gives the wine its signature sparkle.

Other production methods include the ***Ancestral Method*** and the similar (and currently trendy) ***Pétillant Naturel*** (Pét-Nat), where the wine is bottled before it finishes primary fermentation, and it is left unfiltered. This results in a cloudy and somewhat funky sparkling wine. In the glass, these may look and taste almost like cider or sour beer. There are also sparkling wines produced by force carbonation (where the wine is injected with CO_2). These wines will have more aggressive bubbles, not unlike soda pop, and we don't recommend them.

Now that we've set the ground rules, let's take a closer look at the two main production methods – Traditional versus Charmat. We will also break down these methods in greater detail later in Chapter 7 (by which time you'll be an effervescent expert).

Traditional Method vs. Charmat Method

Also known as Méthode Traditionnelle, Classic Method or Méthode Champenoise.	Also known as Cuve Close Method, Tank Method, Metodo Martinotti or Metodo Italiano.
Secondary fermentation occurs in bottle.	Secondary fermentation occurs in a stainless-steel tank.
This is a lengthy process that can take nine months to five years or more.	This is a quick process that typically takes less than six weeks.
After the secondary fermentation is complete, the wine is left to age in bottle to develop complexity. The length of aging time is dependent upon the desired final product.	After the secondary fermentation in the tank, the wine is bottled and sent to market.
The resulting wines are rich and complex. The carbonation is more vigorous, with finer bubbles and a distinctive brioche note.	The resulting wines are fresh and aromatic. The carbonation is softer, with larger bubbles, and a fruit-forward nature.
These wines should usually be enjoyed within one to three years of being purchased, however some high-quality examples can improve further with age.	These wines should be enjoyed while young, within a year of being purchased, and will not improve with age.

Traditional Method: *Secondary fermentation occurs in bottle.*

Charmat Method: *Secondary fermentation occurs in a pressurized stainless-steel tank.*

Styles of Sparkling Wine Based on Sweetness

Sugar in wine can be an unsavoury topic. Whether you're counting your carbs or calories, or you just want to know what's in your glass while on your journey to find your sparkle, sweetness is an important, but often confusing, aspect of sparkling wine.

One of the main ways to assess and classify sparkling wine is by the amount of **residual sugar** (RS) it contains (measured in grams per litre). To achieve a desired level of sweetness in a sparkling wine, a **dosage** (a mixture of sugar and still wine) is typically added to the wine (some wines have no dosage added, however).

While there may not be anything confusing about sugar itself, the terms used to describe sweetness can throw you off your game. Let's introduce you to the sweetness scale to help you navigate this luscious topic.

- **Brut Nature** (also called Brut Zero): Up to 3 grams per litre of residual sugar. Not sweet at all.

- **Extra Brut**: Up to 6 grams per litre of residual sugar. Barely sweet.

- **Brut**: Up to 12 grams per litre of residual sugar. By far the most common style of sparkling wine. What most would classify as the traditional definition of "dry" (not sweet) when referring to wine, but with just a kiss of sugar to help round out the wine's naturally high acidity.

- **Extra Dry** (also Extra Sec or Extra Secco): 12 to 17 grams per litre of residual sugar. This is where things get confusing, as many might think "Extra Dry" means "Extra Brut" when it actually means "sweeter than dry." You will likely perceive some sweetness in these wines.

- **Dry** (also Sec or Secco): 17 to 32 grams per litre of residual sugar. Another confusing term, as "Dry" really means sweet in this case.

- **Demi-Sec** (also Semi-Secco): 32 to 50 grams per litre of residual sugar. We are approaching dessert wine territory.

- **Doux**: 50+ grams per litre of residual sugar. The sweetest sparkling wine style is often meant to be enjoyed alongside dessert or as a dessert itself.

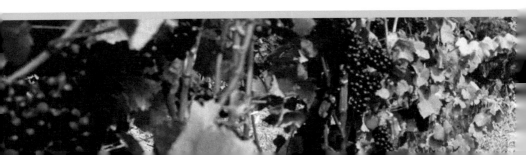

Styles of Sparkling Wine Based on Grape Variety

Another important way to classify sparkling wine is by grape variety or varieties used in its production.

Common varieties include Chardonnay, Pinot Noir, Pinot Meunier, Pinot Blanc, Chenin Blanc, Riesling, Pinot Gris, Sauvignon Blanc, Merlot, Cabernet Franc, Glera, Lambrusco, Macabeo, Parellada and Xarel·lo.

Sparkling wines can be labelled by a single variety (Chardonnay, for example), but they are more often made from a blend of different grape varieties. When a blend, or ***cuvée***, is used to make sparkling wine, you may not see a grape variety named on the main label, though some producers may list them on the back label.

Other common labelling terms for sparkling wine include:

- **Brut**: Although this term is an indicator of sweetness level and has nothing to do with grape variety, many producers will use the word on a bottle to denote a white sparkling wine made in the Brut style (less than 12 grams per litre of residual sugar), from a blend of different grape varieties (with Chardonnay and Pinot Noir being the most popular).

- **Rosé**: Quite simply, a pink sparkling wine! There are two different ways to add a splash of pink to bubbles: either by simply adding a small amount of still red wine as part of the dosage or by allowing the juice to remain in contact with red grape skins for a short period before fermentation to soak up some colour.

- ***Blanc de Blancs***: Translates to "White from Whites," meaning a white sparkling wine made only from white grapes. Typically Chardonnay, but it can be made from any white grapes. These wines usually show more tree fruit, citrus, and floral notes.

- ***Blanc de Noirs***: Translates to "White from Blacks," meaning a white sparkling wine made from black (or red) grapes – typically Pinot Noir and/or Pinot Meunier – pressed gently to avoid skin contact. It's important to note that although the skins of the grapes are red, the juice is clear (or white). These wines usually have a bit more structure and hints of red fruit.

HOW SWEET IS YOUR SPARKLE?

Brut Nature
Bone Dry

Extra Brut
Very Dry

Brut
Dry

0 - 3 g/L

0 - 6 g/L

0 - 12 g/L

Ranges from
0 to less than 1
cube of sugar
per litre.

Ranges from
0 to less than 1.5
cubes of sugar
per litre.

Ranges from
0 to less than 3
cubes of sugar
per litre.

That's less than
1/6 of a teaspoon
of sugar per glass.

That's less than
1/4 of a teaspoon
of sugar per glass.

That's less than
1/2 of a teaspoon
of sugar per glass.

Extra Dry	**Dry**	**Demi-Sec**	**Doux**
Medium Dry	*Medium Sweet*	*Sweet*	*Very Sweet*

12 - 17 g/L	**17 - 32 g/L**	**32 - 50 g/L**	**50+ g/L**
Ranges from 3 to 4 cubes of sugar per litre.	Ranges from 4 to 8 cubes of sugar per litre.	Ranges from 8 to 12 cubes of sugar per litre.	Contains 12 cubes of sugar or more per litre.
That's between 1/2 to 3/4 of a teaspoon of sugar per glass.	That's between 3/4 to 1 teaspoon of sugar per glass.	That's between 1 to 2 teaspoons of sugar per glass.	That's more than 2 teaspoons of sugar per glass.

Chapter 2:

READING IS FUNDAMENTAL

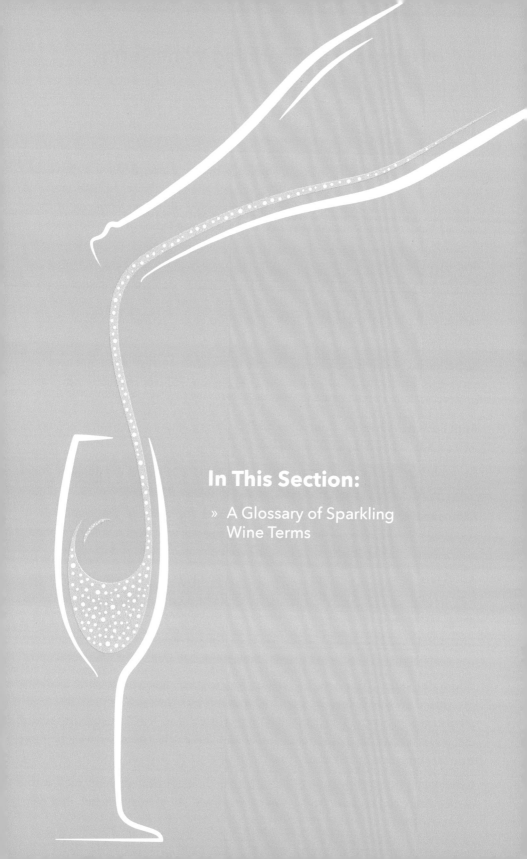

In This Section:

» A Glossary of Sparkling
Wine Terms

A Glossary of Sparkling Wine Terms

Rather than end the book with a glossary of terms, we thought it made way more sense to include it early on. This way, we can ensure that we're all on the same page and speaking the same language.

If you come across a word that you're unfamiliar with at any time throughout this book, flip back here and refresh your vocabulary. Pretty soon, you'll be deciphering wine labels like a pro and seriously impressing your sommelier when they plop one of those intimidating binder-like restaurant wine lists down in front of you!

- **Ancestral Method**: A method of production used to make sparkling wine in which it undergoes a single, in-bottle fermentation during which the bubbles are produced and trapped. This production method can be risky and challenging to control, with significant bottle variation. Can also be referred to as the Méthode Ancestrale or *Pétillant Naturel.*

- **Appellation**: A defined geographical area in the production of wine that is subject to various production and winemaking regulations. There are many *appellation* systems worldwide, including the French *AOC* and Italian *DOC.*

- **Appellation d'Origine Contrôlée (AOC)**: A regulatory system that applies to wines made in prescribed regions in France.

- **Assemblage**: A winemaking term, that when used for sparkling winemaking, refers to the act of assembling (blending) still base wines to create a *cuvée.*

- **Atmosphere**: A unit of measure used to assess the pressure inside a bottle of sparkling wine. *Traditional Method* sparkling wines will typically have 6 atmospheres of pressure, while sparkling wines made in other methods will often have less.

- **Autolysis**: A winemaking term used to describe the process where toasty, biscuit-like and creamy characters develop in sparkling wines that age *sur lie* (on their *lees*).

- **Blanc de Blancs**: Translates to "White from Whites," meaning a white sparkling wine made only from white grapes. Typically Chardonnay, but it can be made from any white grapes. These wines usually show more tree fruit, citrus and floral notes.

- **Blanc de Noirs**: Translates to "White from Blacks," meaning a white sparkling wine made from black (or red) grapes – typically Pinot Noir and/or Pinot Meunier – pressed gently to avoid skin contact. It's important to note that although the skins of the grapes are red, the juice is clear (or white). These wines usually have a bit more structure and hints of red fruit.

- **Brix**: A standardized measure of sugar content in unfermented grape juice, with 1 degree Brix (°Bx) equating to 1 gram of sugar per 100 grams of liquid. Brix helps winemakers estimate grape maturity and potential alcohol. Grapes intended for sparkling wine are commonly picked at lower Brix (approximately 17.5-18 Brix) compared to those intended for table wine.

- **Cage**: Describes the twisted wire used to keep a capped cork in place on a bottle of sparkling wine. It can also be called a muselet.

- **Cava**: A *Traditional Method* sparkling wine from northeastern Spain.

- **Charmat Method**: A method of production used to make sparkling wine that results from a secondary fermentation in a large, pressurized stainless steel tank. It may also be called the Cuve Close Method, Tank Method, Metodo Martinotti or Metodo Italiano.

- **Champagne**: A *Traditional Method* sparkling wine from northeastern France.

- **Comité interprofessionnel du vin de Champagne (CIVC)**: A trade organization bringing together the growers, cooperatives, and merchants of Champagne, under the direction of the French government.

- **Coupe**: A stemmed wine glass with a wide-shallow shape. It may also be referred to as a Champagne Saucer.

- **Crémant**: Originally meaning "creamy," this term applies to a group of *Traditional Method* sparkling wines made in several French *AOCs*, but outside of Champagne.

- **Cuvée**: A blend of still base wines used to make sparkling wine.

- **Denominación de Origen (DO)**: A regulatory system that applies to wines made in prescribed regions in Spain.

- **Denominazione di Origine Controllata (DOC)**: A regulatory system that applies to wines made in prescribed regions in Italy. The superior classification to DOC in Italy is Denominazione di Origine Controllata e Garantita (DOCG), meaning controlled and guaranteed designation of origin.

- **Disgorgement**: Removing *lees* from the neck of a bottle of sparkling wine, which follows *riddling*.

- **Dosage**: The addition of the *liqueur d'expédition* (sugar and still wine) after *disgorgement* (in the *Traditional Method*) or before bottling (in the *Charmat Method*) to achieve a desired level of sweetness. It is optional, and some sparkling wines have no dosage.

- **Esters**: Organic acids that are aromatic and occur during the fermentation process in wine. There are hundreds of esters that may be perceived. Unlike esters – which are a result of fermentation – the other aroma compounds in wine (such as terpenes, thiols, pyrazines and norisoprenoids) originate from the grape.

- **Fermentation**: The process of *yeast* converting sugar to alcohol and carbon dioxide. In *Traditional Method* sparkling wine, as a result of secondary fermentation, the carbon dioxide is trapped in the bottle, creating its signature effervescence.

- **Flute**: A stemmed wine glass with a narrow-tall shape.

- **Franciacorta**: *Traditional Method* sparkling wine from northern Italy.

- **Frizzante**: A lighter, less effervescent style of sparkling wine.

- **Grande Marque**: In Champagne, this term refers to over 20 large and world-famous *Maisons* (Champagne Houses).

- **Grower Champagne**: In Champagne, this refers to wines produced by growers and grower-cooperatives in ways that reflect and respect local *terroir* and vineyard sites, showcasing unique qualities. May also be referred to in French as Les Champagnes de Vignerons.

- **Gyropalette**: A piece of equipment used in the production of *Traditional Method* sparkling wine that automates and speeds up the process of *riddling*.

- **Icewine**: A lusciously sweet, concentrated style of wine, made from grapes naturally frozen on the vine. Made chiefly in Canada, it is also found in Germany, where it is called Eiswein.

- **Lambrusco**: A sparkling red wine from northern Italy.

- **Lees**: Refers to the dead *yeast* cells that remain in the bottle following fermentation. Wine that ages *sur lie* (on the *lees*) will benefit from *autolysis*.

- **Liqueur d'Expédition**: A blend of wine and sugar added to a *Traditional Method* sparkling wine after *disgorgement*.

- **Maison**: In Champagne, this French term for "house" is typically used to refer to a winery.

- **Méthode Cap Classique**: *Traditional Method* sparkling wine from South Africa, often shortened to MCC.

- **Millésimé**: A French labelling term referring to a *vintage*-dated wine.

- **Minerality**: A wine descriptor referring to the mineral character in a sparkling wine, which may include chalk, wet stone and salinity.

- **Mousse**: This French term for "foam" refers to the frothy layer on top of a just-poured glass of sparkling wine.

- **Must**: Refers to freshly pressed, unfermented grape juice.

- **Non-Vintage**: A labelling term used to describe sparkling wine made from a blend of multiple wines from various years.

- **Perlage**: This French term for "beadwork" refers to the effervescence of a sparkling wine as it appears in the glass.

- **Pétillant Naturel (Pét-Nat)**: See *Ancestral Method*.

- **Prosecco**: *Charmat Method* sparkling wine from northeastern Italy.

- **Residual Sugar**: The natural grape sugars (measured in grams per litre) that remain in a wine after fermentation is complete. Residual sugar levels vary in different types of wines.

- **Riddling**: A process of positioning a bottle of sparkling wine that allows the *lees* to settle in the neck of the bottle, allowing for efficient *disgorgement*. May also be referred to as remuage.

- **Sabrage**: The art of opening a bottle of sparkling wine with a sabre or sword. While it can be dangerous (and inefficient due to the loss of sparkling wine), it can be super fun! See Chapter 3 for details.

- **Sekt**: Sparkling wine from Germany (and Austria).

- **Spumante**: An Italian term for sparkling wine.

- **Sur Lie**: A French term meaning "on the *lees*" (dead *yeast* cells).

- **Terroir**: A fancy word for a "sense of place." It's the combination of a particular region's climate, soils and terrain, and how they affect the taste of the wine.

- **Tirage**: The addition of sugar and *yeast* to a bottle of base wine, igniting the secondary *fermentation*.

- **Traditional Method**: A method of production used to make sparkling wine through a secondary fermentation in bottle. Also called the Méthode Traditionnelle or Méthode Champenoise.

- **Trentodoc**: An *appellation* and *Traditional Method* sparkling wine from northeastern Italy.

- **Vintage**: A labelling term used to describe sparkling wine for which 100% of grapes come from the noted year. *Vintage* wines are typically only made in exceptional growing years. See *Millésimé*.

- **Vintners Quality Alliance (VQA)**: A regulatory and *appellation* system used for Canadian wines.

- **Vitis vinifera**: Also referred to as the European wine grape or common grape, this species is the most cultivated and widely used for winemaking across the globe. You may also encounter Vitis labrusca or hybrid grape varieties in some markets.

- **Yeast**: See *Lees*.

Chapter 3:

UNDER PRESSURE

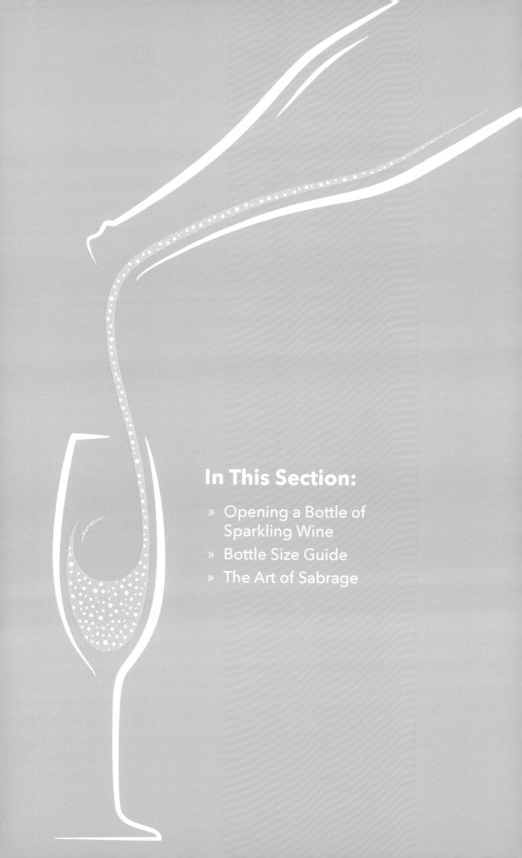

In This Section:

Opening a Bottle of Sparkling Wine

Many people are intimidated when it comes to opening a sparkling wine … and for good reason, as each bottle contains a significant amount of pressure.

A bottle of Champagne, and other Traditional Method sparkling wines, will typically contain about 6 *atmospheres* of pressure. Prosecco, and other wines made in the Charmat Method, will normally have less pressure, about 3.5 atmospheres per bottle. Unless you're a physicist, units of measure associated with pressure can be … nebulous, at best. For some helpful context, an average car tire contains just over 2 atmospheres. This illustrates the point that, yes, there is much pressure inside that glass bottle of bubbly, so you should be careful when handling and opening it!

Fear not, though, for we will pull you down from the pressure up there in the sparkling wine atmosphere. If you follow these eight simple steps, you'll be safely popping bottles like a pro, with careful consideration for yourself and the bubbleheads around you.

So, what should you do to safely open and enjoy a bottle of sparkling wine?

1. **Make sure that the bottle is cold**. If the bottle is too warm, the pressure inside will be more volatile and can cause the cork to release too quickly or unexpectedly. The bottle should be chilled down to about 7°C (or 45°F). You can achieve this by either leaving the bottle in the fridge for at least three hours; giving it an ice bath (putting it into an ice bucket with a 50/50 mix of ice cubes and water) for about 30 minutes; or by putting it into a freezer for about 45 minutes. Don't worry, placing a bottle of wine in the freezer isn't going to impact its taste (that's an old wives' tale), just don't forget about it, or you'll end up with a wine slushy. Trust us. We've been there.

2. **Remove the foil**. If the wine was in an ice bath, ensure you dry off the bottle with a kitchen towel so that it doesn't slip out of your hands. Most sparkling wine bottles will have a tab or perforation somewhere along the foil to help you remove it easily. If not, just go nuts and tear it off.

3. **Loosen the *cage***. Untwist the wire six times and then loosen the cage all the way around the bottle but DO NOT remove it. This life hack will do wonders for your safe enjoyment of sparkling wine and it is, unfortunately, where many people go wrong. We can't tell you the number of times we've seen someone remove the cage entirely, waving the bottle around, without a care in the world. The cage is your friend and will act as a safety grip, allowing you to manage the pressure in the bottle (and prevent the cork from shooting off like a bullet at any moment).

4. **Keep your thumb on top of the cork**. In addition to the cage, your thumb acts as an extra layer of protection should the cork unexpectedly pop.

5. **Pick up the bottle and hold it at a 45° angle**, with the base firmly in your non-dominant hand. Hold the cork (with the loosened cage on top) firmly in your dominant hand.

6. **Twist the base of the bottle, NOT the cork**. Slowly twist the base of the bottle while keeping a firm grip on the cork. Do not twist the cork, as it may break inside the bottle. You'll start to feel the cork become dislodged from the bottle.

7. **Aim for a hiss, not a POP**! The slower you remove the cork from the bottle, the quieter the climax will be. When you feel like the cork is about to separate from the bottle, put a little bit of pressure down against it and gently wiggle it out. Despite the pop being a festive addition to any celebration, traditional serving practice suggests you try and get the cork out with as little noise as possible.

8. **Clean the lip of the bottle and enjoy**! Occasionally you may see some small cork particles on the lip of the bottle after opening it. Give it a quick wipe with a kitchen towel, pour the wine into your favourite vessel, and enjoy.

Step 1: *Make sure that the bottle is cold.*

Step 2: *Remove the foil.*

Step 5: *Pick up the bottle and hold it at a 45° angle.*

Step 6: *Twist the base of the bottle, NOT the cork.*

Step 3: *Loosen the cage but DO NOT remove it.*

Step 4: *Keep your thumb on top of the cork.*

Step 7: *Aim for a **hiss**, not a **POP**!*

Step 8: *Clean the lip of the bottle, and enjoy!*

Quarter Bottle (187 mL) 1/4 bottle

Half Bottle (375 mL) 1/2 bottle

Standard Bottle (750 mL) 1 bottle

Magnum (1.5 L) 2 bottles

Jeroboam (3 L) 4 bottles

Rehoboam (4.5 L) 6 bottles

Methuselah (6 L) 8 bottles

Salmanazar (9 L) 12 bottles

Balthazar (12 L) 16 bottles

Nebuchadnezzar (15 L)
20 bottles

Solomon (18 L)
24 bottles

Sovereign (26.25 L)
35 bottles

Primat (27 L)
36 bottles

Melchizedek (30 L)
40 bottles

BOTTLE SIZE GUIDE

The Art of Sabrage

We've covered the proper way to open a bottle of sparkling wine. But there is another way that's just a little bit more fun and it's called the art of Sabrage or, to put it simply, **opening a bottle of sparkling wine with a sword like a kick-ass samurai**.

If you don't conveniently have a sabre laying around at home, you can use the blunt (back) edge of a chef's knife instead. But we always say … a house is not a home without a sabre!

Disclaimer: This is for demonstration purposes only, and we don't recommend trying this at home unless you are in the hands of a professional and in a safe, well-lit space that is clear from people, pets and objects; and you are wearing the proper protective gear and are clear of any encumbrances. Remember, sparkling wine is volatile and safety comes first!

Sabrage is one cool party trick and a ritual synonymous with celebration. We've been hired all over to perform it, and we've got it down to a science we'll share with you. To safely and successfully execute a Sabrage, all you must remember is our handy **T-A-S-T-E** system.

1. **T is for Temperature**: This is a critical step and is the foundation for a successful Sabrage. Make sure your sparkling wine has been in the fridge for at least three hours or in an ice bath for 30 minutes or more, preferably with the neck down. The colder the neck of the bottle is, the better (just make sure it's not frozen)!

2. **A is for Angle**: Tear off the foil and carefully remove the cage (ensuring the bottle is directed away from people and objects at all times). Now hold the bottle at a 45° angle, gripping the base firmly in your non-dominant hand. You'll hold your sword in your dominant hand.

3. **S is for Seam**: Locate the seam of the bottle. Each bottle has two (one on either side). As part of this step, make sure that any extra foil or labels along the neck are removed so they don't get in your way.

4. **T is for Tap**: Are you ready? While holding the bottle at 45°, ensure that your sabre is lying flush to the bottle. Glide the blade up along the seam and tap the lip of the bottle with a gentle force (as if you are throwing a frisbee). The goal is for the neck of the bottle to break cleanly at the lip, with the cork and a portion of the glass bottle neck being expelled. Like temperature, your tap is critical, so make sure you don't hit too hard as you'll experience some disappointment!

5. **E is for Enjoy**: See how easy that was? Now ENJOY your bubbles, and we can pretty much guarantee that you'll never want to open a bottle of sparkling wine any other way! When handling the cork or bottle after Sabrage, be careful of any sharp edges.

T is for Temperature:

Make sure that the bottle is cold.

A is for Angle:

Hold the bottle at a 45° angle.

E is for Enjoy:

Enjoy your bubbles (and new skill)!

S is for Seam:

Locate the seam of the bottle.

T is for Tap:

Tap the lip of the bottle.

Chapter 4:

LET'S TASTE, SHALL WE?

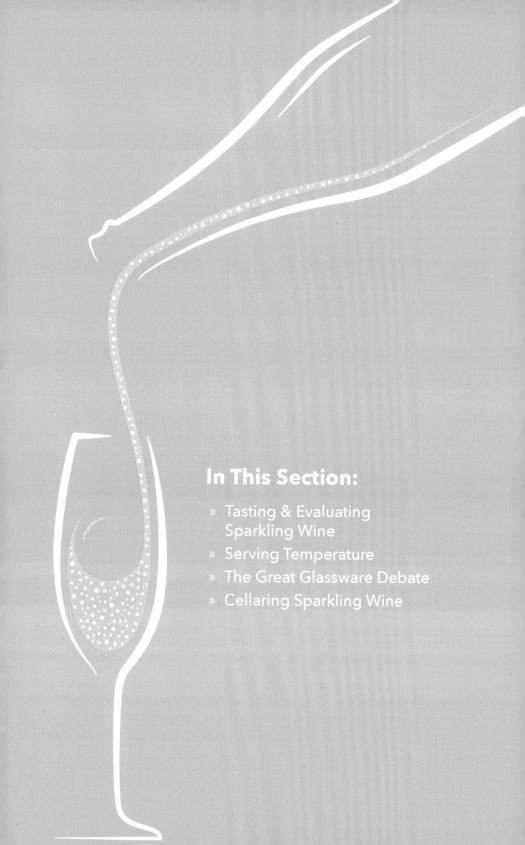

In This Section:

Tasting & Evaluating Sparkling Wine

It may seem ridiculous for us to tell you "how to taste" wine, as taste is subjective and **your sparkling wine journey is unique to you**. You put a glass to your lips and sip, and you taste, right? Well, yes. But wine is a layered and complex libation, and it should be no surprise that tasting and evaluating it is too.

In this chapter, we will share a few tips and tricks to get the most out of your tasting experience and help you begin thinking about sparkling wine more critically.

Now that you know how to open a bottle of bubbly properly (Chapter 3), the other factors to consider are the temperature of the wine and the vessel you're going to pour it into. Once the wine leaves the bottle, its new home in your glass can impact your taste buds much more than you might think!

Serving Temperature

Sparkling wines taste best well chilled.

We recommend serving Charmat Method wines between 4 - 7° Celsius (40 - 45° Fahrenheit) to preserve their freshness and fruitiness. Traditional Method wines should be served between 6 - 10° Celsius (43 - 50° Fahrenheit) to allow their more complex characteristics to shine through. These cooler temperatures slow down the release of carbon dioxide in the wine, causing the bubbles to become finer and rise more slowly in the glass. If sparkling wine is served too warm, it becomes frothy and loses its elegance. You will also want to avoid serving any type of sparkling wine too cold, as this will mute its aromatic profile.

We'd like to talk about your fridge and what it's good for – other than storing your leftovers! Timing is everything when storing sparkling wine in your refrigerator. With the average refrigerator temperature being 4° Celsius (40° Fahrenheit), it will take a bottle of room temperature sparkling wine about three hours to reach the ideal serving temperatures we have outlined above.

If you didn't plan that far ahead, you can also chill your bottle of sparkling in the freezer for about 45 minutes (without negatively impacting the profile of the wine). Or do it the way the pros do, and give your sparkling wine an ice bath (a 50/50 mix of ice cubes and water in an ice bucket) for about 30 minutes.

The Great Glassware Debate

The **flute** is synonymous with sparkling wine and celebration. It's the vessel of choice for most people when serving their bubbles. But guess what? As with most things in life, just because something is the most popular doesn't mean it's the best. While the flute's narrow-but-tall shape does an excellent job of preserving the precious bubbles in the glass, it also limits your sensory experience. The narrow opening does not allow for much oxygen to penetrate the wine – oxygen that helps release the wine's delicate aromas. As a result, flutes should be avoided when serving richer and more complex styles of sparkling wine (such as Champagne, *Franciacorta* or other Traditional Method wines). We've often heard, and ourselves repeated, that serving Champagne in a flute is like going to a concert while wearing earplugs. You'll be missing out on the full experience. If you're devoted to enjoying your bubbles from a flute, we recommend a simple and more fruit-forward style of sparkling wine (such as Prosecco, Asti, or other Charmat Method wines).

On the other end of the spectrum is the ***coupe***. Vintage in its style, it has an old-Hollywood charm and certainly makes for a great party favour. However, its wide-but-shallow shape produces drawbacks that are opposite to those of the flute. The wide opening results in the bubbles dissipating more quickly, causing the wine to taste softer because there is less pronounced effervescence on the palate. While the flute doesn't allow enough oxygen in to permit the aromatics to fully develop, the coupe allows too much oxygen in. The aromas dissipate without being captured and appreciated. But it's not all opposites: like the flute, the coupe is best reserved for simpler fruit-forward styles of sparkling wine (such as Prosecco, Asti, or other Charmat Method wines) and not used for richer and complex styles, with a deeper breadth of aromas and flavours (such as Champagne, Franciacorta, or other Traditional Method wines).

We say life is all about compromise and thankfully, in this debate, we can meet in the middle. The perfect glassware option for sparkling wine – and odds are you already have it in your kitchen cabinet – is the humble **white wine glass**. With its tall shape, narrow (but not too narrow) opening and smaller bowl, it offers the perfect conditions to preserve a sparkling wine's bubbles (as the flute does). It also ensures that the bubbles will not dissipate too quickly (as happens with the coupe). The bowl of the white wine glass is wide enough to allow oxygen in to mingle with and release the aromas of the wine (unlike the flute), but it's narrow enough to trap these aromas so you can enjoy them more intensely (unlike the coupe). The white wine glass is the ace up your sleeve when it comes to serving and enjoying sparkling wine. All styles of sparkling wine shine in this vessel, and we think it's a must if you're serving premium or aged styles of sparkling.

Another option to consider is the **tulip glass**, which we see as the happy medium between the classic flute and the white wine glass. Life is all about nuance, right? It differs from the flute with its wider, flared bowl and tapered opening, which allows for full aroma appreciation but prevents the unnecessarily fast loss of carbonation. After all, you want to appreciate those bubbles in the glass. The tulip glass is also an elegant, specialty option – we think your guests will be impressed!

However, as with all things wine, glassware is subjective and, at the end of the day, the choice is yours.

Wine is all about choosing your own adventure. So next time you pop a bottle of bubbly, try out the different types of glassware and see for yourself if you experience a contrast in aromatics and on the palate. Hey, it's a good excuse to treat yourself to that second glass.

The Flute Glass

Preserves effervescence. Suitable for fruity, easy-going sparkling wines (such as Prosecco).

The Coupe Glass

A stylish and fun party favour! Suitable for fruity, easy-going sparkling wines (such as Prosecco).

The White Wine Glass

Enhances aromatics. Suitable for richer, more complex sparkling wines (such as Champagne).

The Tulip Glass

A happy medium! Suitable for richer, more complex sparkling wines (such as Champagne).

Cellaring Sparkling Wine

People often ask us: "Should I drink this wine now or wait a few years?"

Contrary to what many people think, **most sparkling wine is not meant to age in your cellar**. About 90% of sparkling wines are meant to be enjoyed while young and fresh. Wines that are vibrant and fruit-forward in style (such as Prosecco) will not improve with age; they will only deteriorate. These wines should be enjoyed within 6 - 12 months of being bottled. About 10% of wines (higher quality examples, such as Champagne or other Traditional Method wines) can age, but keep in mind they will change over time.

While a *non-vintage* Traditional Method wine, created by blending several still reserve wines from different vintages (or years), is intended to be enjoyed close to its *disgorgement* date, it can be cellared successfully for up to five years. A *vintage* Traditional Method wine, created from grapes sourced from a single harvest (and only in exceptional growing years) will likely be aged for some time before being released. These wines will have a year indicated on the label, and may also be called *Millésimé*, if made in France. They can be cellared for up to 10 years, but exceptional Millésimé are built to last in the cellar and may be aged longer. Some producers will include the disgorgement date on the label, which we think is the most valuable guide for enjoying and cellaring wine.

So, what can you expect when aging sparkling wines?

The acidity will slowly fade, the bubbles will become less pronounced, and the fruity character will evolve to a more baked-fruit flavour, with distinctive nutty and honeyed notes (often called tertiary character). An aged, vintage Champagne is certainly something to behold (and a style that we love), but these wines are not for everyone and may not be appropriate for every occasion. If you prefer a brighter and fresher style of sparkling wine, it's best not to hold on to your bottles for too long.

If you plan on cellaring sparkling wine, make sure that it is stored on its side in a cool, dry place with a consistent ambient temperature; and that it is away from vibration and natural light. We don't recommend the age-old practice of storing sparkling wine in your fridge for extended periods. The cold temperature inside your fridge will cause the cork to contract, causing your sparkling wine to experience premature oxidation and potentially a loss of its effervescence. We also don't recommend that you store your wine upright for long periods either. Storing your bubbly upright may cause the cork to dry out, again exposing the sparkling wine to premature oxidation.

> The more wines you taste and explore, the easier it becomes to pick the perfect wine for any occasion, situation or food pairing!

Tasting – An Overview

When tasting and evaluating a sparkling wine, we're going to put our senses to work and look at four key categories:

- **Appearance**: How the wine looks
- **Nose**: How the wine smells
- **Palate**: How the wine tastes
- **Conclusions**: Combining the three categories above to make your assessment of the wine

We're going to break down each of these steps momentarily, but first, here are a few things to consider when tasting …

People often ask us: "If wine is made from grapes, how come I smell and taste apples?" We think this is a fantastic question, leading us (and the taster) to a great conversation about the diversity of sparkling wine. The simple reason for this observation is that while wine is indeed made from grapes, you can find hundreds of aromas and flavours in it due to chemical compounds called *esters*. These compounds are created when the grapes are fermented into wine, and in simple terms, they are identical to those found in fruits, vegetables, and other plants. So, if you pick up on an "apple note" in your glass of sparkling, it may be because the wine contains the same chemical compound found in apples. Differences in grape varieties, fermentation *yeasts*, and winemaking techniques (like aging the wine in oak barrels) all impact the way these chemical compounds manifest as aromas and flavours in your glass of sparkling wine.

With so many aromas and flavours to be discovered with each sip of sparkling wine, it can be overwhelming, but also oh so exciting. As you travel on your personal wine journey exploring the sparkling spectrum, don't be scared to trust your observations and judgement. Be forthright with your thoughts and opinions on what you perceive in your glass of sparkling wine, as it's all highly subjective and uniquely personal. If you smell or taste something in a wine, let it be known, and chances are your tasting partner, or the company you're with, may very well respond with "OMG! Yes, that's it!"

We'd like to pass on to you another bit of sage wine tasting advice: Start building up a database of aromas and flavours in your brain. Of course, we all know what apples smell and taste like, but have a look at our guide on the following page and acquaint yourself with some of the aromas and flavours that you may not be so familiar with. This will be a great help when it comes to honing your nose and palate and will be helpful to you on your sparkling wine journey!

Fruit

Tree & Vine Fruit   Apple, Apricot, Fig, Melon, Nectarine, Peach, Pear, Plum, Quince

Citrus   Citrus Zest, Grapefruit, Lemon, Lime

Berries   Black Cherry, Cranberry, Red and White Currants, Raspberry, Strawberry, White Cherry

Floral & Mineral

Floral   Acacia, Apple Blossom, Honeysuckle, Peach Blossom, Rose

Mineral   Chalk, Flint, Slate, Smoke, Stone

AROMAS & FLAVOURS

Yeast

Pastry   Almond Tart, Biscuit, Brioche, Croissant, Fresh Bread, Toast

Dairy   Butter, Cream, Custard, Parmesan

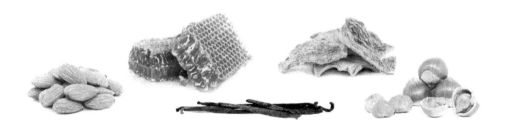

Nuts & Spices

Nuts   Almond, Hazelnut, Pine Nut, Walnut

Spices   Baking Spice, Burnt Sugar, Candied Fruit, Caramel, Honey, Ginger, Gingerbread, Vanilla

Tasting - Appearance

The first step in tasting and evaluating sparkling wine is analyzing its appearance. Take into consideration the following three key categories:

1. **Clarity**: Take a look at the wine. Is it clear or hazy? Most sparkling wine is clear, but unfiltered styles (like Pét-Nat) may appear hazy in the glass.

2. **Colour**: How would you describe the colour of the wine? White sparkling wines usually fall between pale straw and deep gold in colour. Rosés are generally somewhere between pale pink and deep salmon. A lighter colour may indicate a more youthful style of sparkling wine, and a deeper colour may indicate a wine that has spent some time aging.

3. **Bubbles**: Look at the stream of bubbles in the glass. Are they fine, medium or coarse? Fine bubbles are usually a sign of a Traditional Method sparkling wine, medium bubbles usually indicate a Charmat Method sparkling wine, and coarse bubbles are likely a sign that the wine has been force carbonated.

Tasting - Nose

Next, nose (meaning smell) the wine. Either wave or gently tilt the glass under your nose or get your nose right in there and give it a good sniff. Take into consideration the following three key categories:

1. **Condition**: Is the wine clean or unclean? To put it simply, does the wine smell appealing? Or does it smell like it may have gone bad or have a particular fault?

2. **Intensity**: How intense is the aroma of the wine? Is it light, medium or pronounced?

3. **Aromas**: What exactly do you smell in the wine? Make a note of everything that comes to mind. There are three different categories to consider when thinking about aromas:

   I. **Primary**: These aromas come from the grape itself. Primary aromas include things like fruit, floral, herbal and mineral.

   II. **Secondary**: These aromas come from winemaking processes such as fermentation and lees aging. Secondary aromas include yeast, fresh bread, biscuit and butter.

   III. **Tertiary**: These complex aromas result when a wine is cellared properly and aged for an extended period. Tertiary aromas include nuts, honey and baked or candied fruit.

> "If you smell or taste something in a wine, let it be known, and chances are your tasting partner may very well respond with "OMG! Yes, that's it!"

Tasting - Palate

Now for the best part … tasting the wine!

During your first sip, we always say the best approach is to not think about it too much. Enjoy it, assess your first impression, and then ask yourself: "Do I like this wine, and do I want to explore it further?" During your second sip, start to think more critically about the wine and take into consideration these following five key categories:

1. **Sweetness**: How sweet do you perceive the wine to be? Is it bone dry (not sweet at all), dry (barely sweet), off-dry (a little bit sweet), sweet or lusciously sweet (almost syrupy)?

2. **Acidity**: How crisp and fresh is the wine? Is it too acidic, balanced or flabby?

3. **Body**: How "heavy" is the wine on your palate? Is it light, medium or full-bodied?

4. **Character**: What exactly do you taste in the wine? Make a note of everything that comes to mind. Consider the same three categories as aroma: primary, secondary, and tertiary. Do the flavours of the wine match up with the aromas, or do they differ?

5. **Length**: How long does the wine linger on your palate? Does it finish short (disappears almost immediately), medium (lingers for up to 10 seconds) or long (lingers for an extended period)?

Tasting - Conclusions

Finally, we put together all the pieces (appearance, nose and palate) to solve the puzzle. **The key to great sparkling wine is balance**. So, when coming to your conclusion, think about the complete picture: did everything work together, in perfect harmony? Or were there aspects of the wine that fell short or overshadowed others?

Think about the following three categories to reach your conclusion about the wine you tasted:

1. **Method**: How was the wine crafted? Was it made in the Traditional Method, Charmat Method or other?

2. **Origins**: Which grape(s) was the wine made from, and which region did it come from? Pinpointing a region can be difficult, especially with sparkling wine, but the more you taste, the more familiar you will become with specific nuances of particular regions.

3. **Quality**: Taking everything above into consideration, and with balance in mind, how would you rate the quality of the wine? Is it poor, average, good or outstanding?

While this might seem like a lot to digest at first sip, the more you explore and taste on your sparkling wine journey, the quicker and easier it becomes. When you start to think more critically about the wine you are tasting, you will begin to build a database – of aromas, flavours, characteristics, grape varieties, wine styles and regions – that you can refer to. The more wines you taste and explore, the easier it becomes to pick the perfect wine for any occasion, situation or food pairing.

Not only will this tasting guide help you to seriously impress your friends, but it will enable you to confidently make educated decisions when confronted with a binder-like wine list at a restaurant or stacked shelves at your local wine shop!

Chapter 5:

A SOMMELIER'S SECRET WEAPON

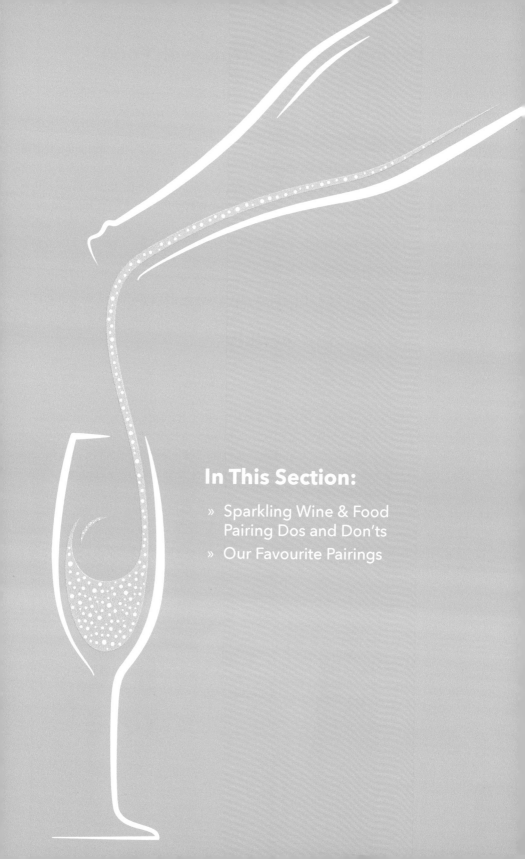

In This Section:

» Sparkling Wine & Food Pairing Dos and Don'ts
» Our Favourite Pairings

Pairing Sparkling Wine with Food

One of life's simplest pleasures is that zen-like sensation of a perfect pairing between food and wine. We aren't the only ones who like to call it a "foodgasm."

Luckily, these are relatively easy to achieve with sparkling wine, as it's **the most versatile and food-friendly wine style out there**. We like to say that it's a sommelier's secret weapon. Thanks to its naturally high palate-cleansing acidity, and its tiny bubbles (that help lift food particles off your tongue, getting you ready for your next bite), it pairs perfectly with pretty much everything. You can serve sparkling wine on its own as an aperitif, with each course of your meal, and even with dessert. So, when in doubt, pop the bubbly!

Let us elaborate on the **four key attributes** that make sparkling wine so food-friendly:

Acidity

Acidity is king when it comes to sparkling wine.

When you first take a sip of wine and experience a tart, mouth-puckering sensation … that's the acidity working its magic. It's the bright and refreshing tingle on your palate that causes your mouth to salivate. It's what lures you in for another sip. When someone describes a sparkling wine as "crisp" or "fresh," they are referring to its acidity.

Acidity is also arguably the most important factor when pairing wine and food. It pierces through rich, salty, fatty and oily foods – all the good stuff – and cleanses your palate, preparing you for your next bite. It's like taking a cold shower after a day in the scorching hot sun. So refreshing!

COMTES
DE CHAMPAGNE
GRANDS CRUS · BLANC DE BLANCS
TAITTINGER
2008

"Some of the best food pairings for sparkling wine are what many would classify as "junk food.""

Bubbles

Like acidity, the bubbles in sparkling wine also refresh your palate. They lift lingering food particles off your tongue and cleanse your palate between bites. The light, fizzy texture also provides a nice contrast to the rich texture of creamy or oily foods, creating a wonderfully satisfying sensation in your mouth.

With both acidity and bubbles working together, sparkling wine is easily the most refreshing and palate-cleansing wine style. This tag-team effect makes sparkling wine the perfect match for pretty much any type of food. It's what makes sparkling a great option for your dinner table when you have a diverse array of dishes and you're looking for a wine to work with everything.

Structure

Several factors contribute to the structure of a wine, including acidity, tannins and alcohol. Sparkling wine is high in acidity, has virtually no tannins (or very little) and is low in alcohol. This results in a refreshing, light- to medium-bodied wine that will complement your food and not overpower it.

In contrast, think about a big, bold Cabernet Sauvignon from California: it's packed with jammy fruit flavour, grippy tannins and is high in alcohol, usually clocking in at 15%. If you poured a glass of this Cab Sauv alongside a delicate, fresh dish like sushi, odds are you wouldn't even taste the sushi. The weight and freshness of sparkling wine, on the other hand, would be quite complementary in the context of this pairing and not at all overpowering.

Character

Just like its structure, the character and flavour profile of sparkling wine lends itself well to working with a diverse range of dishes. Sparkling wine is fruit-forward in nature which, again, contributes to its refreshing character and ability to complement food rather than overpower it. The bubbles in the wine act as magnifying glasses, bringing these flavours to the forefront.

As we said earlier, the sparkling spectrum is broad. And like an ensemble cast, although there is a common thread running through the different styles, many of them have their own special characteristics that really help them shine in a particular role, or in this case, food pairing. And we're going to dig into some of those shortly!

Sparkling Wine & Food Pairing Dos and Don'ts

- **DO**: Keep an open mind and try something new. The beauty of food and wine pairing is discovering new, unique, and interesting flavour combinations.

- **DON'T**: Pair dry wine with dessert. The wine should always be sweeter than the food.

- **DO**: Pair sweeter wine with spicy food. A little bit of sweetness helps to tame the heat in spicy dishes. Steer clear from pairing dry wine with spicy food as this will just accentuate the heat and make the wine difficult to enjoy.

- **DON'T**: Worry! This is supposed to be fun, remember? And sparkling wine pairs with pretty much everything. Just remember the few simple rules above and you'll be good to go!

Fizz Fact: Remember, *what grows together, goes together*. For generations, the people of any given wine region crafted wine to pair with their local cuisine. Think Prosecco and polenta, Lambrusco and pasta Bolognese, Champagne and salty, creamy cheeses ... you get the idea. So, when in doubt (or looking for that perfect pairing), keep this helpful rule in mind!

Hungry yet? Ok, let's get to the meat and potatoes (pun intended) of this chapter and talk about some of our favourite food pairings.

Many people still associate sparkling wine with luxury, celebration and opulence – and these same folks tend to think it can only be enjoyed at special occasions or alongside elegant (often pricey) dishes such as oysters and caviar. As we have seen in our wine journey, this couldn't be further from the truth. While classic pairings such as Champagne and oysters or caviar are rooted in time-tested, age-old culinary tradition (which we appreciate), some of the best food pairings for sparkling wine are what many would classify as "junk food."

We love the idea of "high versus low" – pairing something as elegant as sparkling wine with junk food, or other accessible indulgences. With that in mind, we embarked on some delicious research, to put together a list for you of our favourite "classic" sparkling wine and food pairings, alongside a "junk food" alternative. Which one works better? You be the judge!

High: Truffle Fries vs. Low: Potato Chips

Fried, salty and delicious: both the truffle fries and potato chips are an epic match to nosh on, when poured alongside a glass of sparkling wine.

With the truffle fries, a little shaving of the world's most expensive mushroom will take your fries to the next level. The richness and earthiness of the truffle, coupled with the fatty goodness of the fried potatoes, makes for a decadent pairing that works wonderfully with a Traditional Method Blanc de Noirs. This white sparkling, made from red grape varieties such as Pinot Noir, will typically have the acidity and structure along with a fruity and earthy character to stand up to a big plate of truffle fries.

As for the humble potato chip, stick with good old-fashioned salted chips (bonus points if they're kettle-cut, or if you grabbed them from a vending machine) and pair them with a Blanc de Blancs. The freshness and crisp nature of a Chardonnay-based sparkling will slice right through the oily and salty chips. We must say: a match made in bubbly heaven!

High: Chicken Cordon Bleu vs. Low: Chicken Nuggets

With a crispy, breaded, thinly sliced and rolled chicken breast, around a centre of delicious cheese and ham, and topped with a decadent cream sauce, Chicken Cordon Bleu is one flavourful dish. We think a classic Brut Champagne is quite layered as is this dish, and therefore a great pairing.

It's widely acknowledged within the wine community that fried chicken is the most epic pairing for sparkling wine. The palate-cleansing acidity and bubbles cut right through the fatty richness of the chicken. We agree, and we think this widely accepted viewpoint extends not only to the Chicken Cordon Bleu, but also our "low" option … chicken nuggets. As one of our greatest guilty pleasures, we have to say that hot, oily and salty chicken nuggets are also a perfect pairing for a classic Brut sparkling wine (though the nuggets may not be as layered as a Chicken Cordon Bleu). We would go so far as to say that you haven't lived until you've experienced chicken nuggets, paired with a Brut Champagne. And yes, go ahead and double-dip 'em in the ranch sauce!

High: Oysters vs. Low: Shrimp Tempura

Oysters and Champagne are a classic pairing, and they are a classic for a reason. Oysters tend to be salty, mineral-driven, buttery and creamy. Sound familiar? With its chalky mineral-rich soils, Champagne produces wines with that same imparted profile, which also leans towards creaminess and richness. So, it should come as no surprise that Champagne pairs so well with seafood, as it has its roots (literally) in what once was a sea. You can even perceive hints of this *minerality* (that some describe as "saline-tinged minerality" or "oyster-shell") in a Champagne. The tight and vibrant effervescence in a Brut Champagne complements the smooth and briny body of the oyster perfectly, we would say.

Not into bivalves, or their plump and springy insides (or can't afford a dozen fresh oysters flown in from the east coast, on the half shell)? Don't worry; we feel and see you, and we've got you covered. A bottle of Brut Cava (which also has a distinctive mineral character) and a basket of breaded, deep-fried shrimp tempura will work just as well!

High: Steak au Poivre vs. Low: Cheeseburger

Steak and sparkling wine? Most people don't believe us when we say you can pair sparkling wine with steak. Well, we've put it in print because it's a fact!

Test our hypothesis with Steak au Poivre, a classic French dish of pan-fried filet mignon served in a creamy Cognac and peppercorn sauce. A Traditional Method sparkling Rosé has the power and structure to stand up to this elegant yet remarkably simple and flavourful dish. Its electric acidity cuts through the fats present in your Steak au Poivre, and the fresh, fruit-driven character will complement and not overwhelm the beef (especially if it's served medium).

If you don't feel like getting in touch with your inner Julia Child and the art of French cooking, we think a cheeseburger and bubbles sound divine! Whether you grill it yourself or pick it up from a drive-through window, the combination of seasoned and fatty beef with a melted slice of cheese, served on a toasted bun, is a delicious alternative to the Steak au Poivre, and one with which a glass of Traditional Method sparkling Rosé will shine.

High: Charcuterie Board vs. Low: Frozen Pizza

Sparkling Rosé is an excellent match for a charcuterie board, but have you ever paired your assortment of artfully arranged cured meats and cheeses with a lively Lambrusco? We're not talking about the sickeningly sweet Lambrusco of yesteryear, but rather the fresh, fruity, and dry sparkling red expressions from the Emilia-Romagna region of Italy. This beautiful region in northern Italy is famous for its pork products – including Prosciutto di Parma and Mortadella Bologna – and when enjoyed with the local wines, provides the perfect example of "what grows together, goes together." The bright red fruit character of dry Lambrusco works wonderfully with pork, as well as with sharp and aged cheeses (like Parmigiana Reggiano, which also hails from the region).

Don't feel like spending an arm and a leg on an artisanal deli spread? Don't worry, and grab a frozen pizza, preferably with some pepperoni or other meat on it. We always keep a bunch of frozen pizzas on hand for busy nights and late-night snacks, and you can easily gussy them up with whatever you have in your refrigerator. Enjoy it with a glass of dry Lambrusco – which complements and does not overpower the core ingredients – and reflect on the fact that, hey, your frozen pizza is essentially a de facto charcuterie board anyway.

High: French Macarons vs. Low: Mini Donuts

If you've been paying close attention, you'll remember one of the key wine pairing rules: the wine should always be sweeter than the food.

Many people make the mistake of serving a glass of dry sparkling wine with dessert, and all this is going to do is make your bubbles taste bitter. Look for a Demi-Sec Champagne or another sweet style of sparkling such as Asti.

Whether you're fancy-pants with French macarons or keeping it casual with a box of mini donuts from a nationwide coffee chain, just ensure the wine is sweeter than your sweets and you'll be all set!

Sparkling Wine Dinner Menu

You can absolutely serve sparkling wine throughout your evening – from aperitif to dessert. And yes, you can absolutely serve bubbly all year long, as not only is the wine style diverse and food-friendly, but it is also, in our opinion, the most festive and uplifting. This makes it perfect for periods that need a little extra sparkle (or cool refreshment).

To help you with this effervescent endeavour, we've put together a sample menu based upon our "high versus low" suggestions, taking advantage of a few core principles: achieving balance in the pairing (and not overpowering the food or wine), delving deep into time-honoured culinary traditions or the "what grows together, goes together" philosophy, and our own experience in the kitchen (often with a glass of bubbly in hand).

Though we are guiding you through the menu planning process, we also challenge you to pull from your journey and to come up with your own sparkling wine dinner menu. In doing so, have some fun with it, and use our tips and suggestions, knowing that you don't have to spend hundreds of dollars on wine to have a fabulous dinner party. You can choose from a range of everyday foods to achieve perfect, food-pairing harmony. Focus more on the style of wine (Extra Brut, Blanc de Noirs, Demi-Sec, etc.) and look for budget-friendly options from other regions around the world, and you'll be balling in a budget in no time.

High vs. Low Sample Menu

Aperitif & Hors d'oeuvres	Champagne & Oysters	Cava & Shrimp Tempura
Appetizer	Sparkling Rosé & French Onion Soup	Blanc de Blancs & Crab Cakes
Main Course	Blanc de Blancs & Lobster	Extra Brut & Mac 'n' Cheese
Dessert	Demi-Sec Champagne & Macarons	Asti & Mini Donuts

> " The beauty
> of food and
> wine pairing
> is discovering
> new, unique,
> and interesting
> flavour
> combinations.

Chapter 6:

JUST ADD BUBBLES

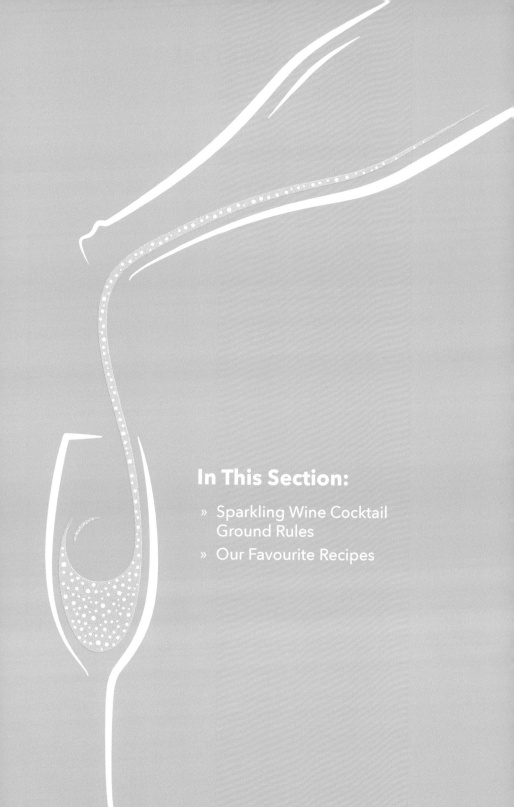

In This Section:

Sparkling Wine Cocktails

What's the key to making an excellent craft cocktail?

Is it a punch of fruit flavour? A dash of thought-provoking complexity? A delicate effervescence? Or … a little "je ne sais quoi"? Well, sparkling wine contains all these things – and is almost like a cocktail all by itself. So, adding a splash of sparkling to your favourite adult beverage can definitely take things to the next level! We believe that bubbly is the key ingredient in crafting the perfect cocktail.

A few ground rules, though:

Don't use Champagne, or another high-end sparkling wine when crafting a sparkling cocktail, as you'll lose a lot of the character in the mix. When it comes to cocktails, which are all about a balance of ingredients and overall profile, any under-$20 bottle of dry sparkling wine will get the job done perfectly. When getting fizzy at the bar cart, an accessible bottle of Cava or a *Crémant* is our usual go-to for mixing in cocktails, as Traditional Method wines will add complexity, a finer bubble, and a bit more structure to the finished product. However, when looking to amplify the fruity nature of a cocktail or to add a kiss of sweetness, Prosecco (or any other Charmat Method sparkling wine) is a great option.

Sparkling cocktails are the perfect ingredient to elevate any festive occasion, whether at the start of a brunch or dinner party, a special celebration, or an epic night out (or, let's face it, in). To help you navigate the endless possibilities, we've compiled a list of our **top 10 favourite recipes**, from fun twists on old-school cocktail classics, to some of our own tried-and-true, mind-blowing secret recipes that we've never shared … until now.

We believe that bubbly is the key ingredient in crafting the perfect cocktail!

Sparkling Blood Orange Margarita

Blood oranges are a bit of a "unicorn," and that's probably why we love them so much. While they are hard to find (and only in season between December and April), they offer a dramatic splash of deep ruby red colour. These elusive, precious fruits are packed not only with colour but with complex flavour – almost like an orange infused with grapefruit or red berries. Match our favourite fruit with the ingredients for a classic margarita, and a splash of Cava to add a bit of extra flair for the holidays – or any other day! Oh, and do yourself a favour and squeeze enough blood oranges for a second round while you're at it. You won't regret it.

Ingredients

- 45 mL (1.5 oz) Silver Tequila
- 15 mL (0.5 oz) orange liqueur (like Cointreau or Grand Marnier)
- 60 mL (2 oz) fresh blood orange juice (about 1 large blood orange, juiced)
- 45 mL (1.5 oz) fresh lime juice (about 1 lime, juiced)
- 5 mL (1 tsp) agave nectar
- 45 mL (1.5 oz) Cava (or other dry sparkling wine)
- Blood orange slice (for garnish)
- Salt (for rim) – optional

Instructions

- Fill a cocktail shaker with ice. Pour in the tequila, orange liqueur, freshly squeezed blood orange juice and lime juice. Don't pour in the Cava or you might end up wearing the cocktail instead!
- Put on the lid and shake vigorously for 20 seconds until chilled and all the ingredients are combined. Strain the liquid into a short cocktail glass, over ice.
- Now, top with the Cava.
- Garnish with a slice of blood orange and enjoy!

Negroni Sbagliato

Classic cocktails are known as such for a reason, and the Negroni has stood the test of time. But just like the movies, classics are often rebooted and reworked. Thankfully, with this example, the reboot might be better than the original, for once.

"Sbagliato" means "mistake" in Italian, and we owe this recipe to Milanese bar owner Mirko Stocchetto who mistakenly reached for a bottle of sparkling wine instead of gin when making a Negroni in the 1970s (grazie mille, Mirko). The result is somewhere in between a classic Negroni and a Spritz. Much richer and more complex than the latter, but lighter than the former. When making these at home, we like to top ours with Prosecco Rosé, which adds a kiss of sweetness and brings out the red berry and cherry notes in the Campari. And hey, it looks pretty in pink too!

Ingredients

- 30 mL (1 oz) sweet vermouth
- 30 mL (1 oz) gin
- 30 mL (1 oz) Campari
- 30 mL (1 oz) Prosecco Rosé
- Orange twist (for garnish)

Instructions

- Combine sweet vermouth, gin and Campari in a short cocktail glass filled with ice. Stir together with a mixing spoon.
- Top with Prosecco Rosé.
- Garnish with an orange twist and enjoy!

Sparkling Bowler

No, this isn't the name of our new bowling league, but rather our take on an iconic French cocktail dating back to the 1930s, called the Champagne Bowler. It's a fresh and fun alternative to sangria, combining three grape-based beverages with muddled strawberries to create an explosive adult fruit punch.

It's also stunningly enticing when served over ice cubes in a large wine glass. And, if you are fortunate enough to have fresh local strawberries in the summertime (as we do here in Southern Ontario), then this is the perfect refreshing summer sipper in place of the much more common Spritz.

Ingredients

- 3 to 4 fresh strawberries, chopped, with the heads removed
- 15 mL (0.5 oz) simple syrup
- 15 mL (0.5 oz) cognac
- 30 mL (1 oz) white wine
- 90 mL (3 oz) dry sparkling wine (Cava, Crémant or Prosecco)
- Strawberry and fresh mint (for garnish)

Instructions

- Muddle the strawberries and simple syrup together in a cocktail shaker. If you don't have a fancy cocktail muddler, a wooden spoon will do the trick!
- Add the cognac and white wine.
- Add ice and shake until chilled. Pour into a large wine glass. Top with sparkling wine.
- Garnish with a strawberry and fresh mint and enjoy!

Prosecco Pineapple Mojito

Few things say "summer" quite like pineapple, Prosecco, and Mojitos (to us, anyway). So we combined our summer favourites to create a super refreshing, fruity and delicately sweet cocktail to complement the summertime vibe (or to help you recreate it on cooler days). And yes, this will likely be your new go-to summer cocktail, so ... you're welcome!

Ingredients

- 4 large fresh mint leaves
- 15 mL (1 tbsp) simple syrup
- 15 mL (1 tbsp) fresh lime juice (about 1/2 of a lime, juiced)
- 90 mL (3 oz) white rum
- 120 mL (4 oz) pineapple juice
- 60 mL (2 oz) Prosecco
- Pineapple wedge and fresh mint (for garnish)

Instructions

- Muddle the fresh mint leaves and simple syrup together in a cocktail shaker. If you don't have a fancy cocktail muddler, a wooden spoon will do the trick!
- Add the white rum, fresh lime juice and pineapple juice.
- Add ice and shake until chilled. Pour into a highball glass. Top with Prosecco.
- Garnish with pineapple wedge and fresh mint and enjoy!

Canadian Royale

In case you missed it, we're Canadian. In this cocktail, we take one of Canada's signatures – *Icewine* – and combine it with sparkling wine in a true-north-strong-and-free twist on the classic Kir Royale. We substitute the Kir for Canada's "liquid gold" which, when topped with sparkling, might as well be liquid platinum, baby!

Behold, the Canadian Royale.

Ingredients

- 120 mL (4 oz) dry sparkling wine (bonus points if it's Canadian)
- 30 mL (1 oz) Canadian Icewine
- Strawberry (for garnish)

Instructions

- Pour the Canadian Icewine into a sparkling wine flute. Hold the glass at a 45-degree angle and gently pour in the sparkling wine.
- Drop a small strawberry into the glass and enjoy!

Sunset Spritz

The Aperol Spritz has been around for over 100 years and has recently seen a massive resurgence in popularity. With its attractive colour, aromatic profile and refreshing, palate-cleansing acidity, it's the perfect pre-dinner drink or summer refresher. Some call it "sunset in a glass." This cocktail's popularity has also brought about its fair share of haters. While we are not among them, we have had a few poorly made examples that diluted, rather than amplified, its simple core ingredients. We substitute complex Campari in place of cheery, fruity Aperol and add a greater proportion of Prosecco. And we use fresh orange juice in place of club soda to boost the fruit-forward nature and captivating colour of this cocktail.

Ingredients

- 60 mL (2 oz) Campari (or Aperol for a slightly sweeter, less herbaceous taste)
- 90 mL (3 oz) Prosecco
- 30 mL (1 oz) fresh orange juice
- Orange slice (for garnish)

Instructions

- Fill a large wine glass with ice.
- Add the Campari and orange juice. Top with Prosecco.
- Garnish with an orange slice and enjoy!

Pink Grapefruit Mimosa

We couldn't put together a list of our favourite sparkling cocktail recipes without including our take on the most famous of all – the Mimosa!

We think a humble Mimosa is great, but we gave the classic brunch cocktail a hot pink makeover. Swapping out a classic Brut sparkling for a sparkling Rosé and switching out orange juice for Ruby Red grapefruit juice, our Pink Grapefruit Mimosa is a tangier take on the original, with a hint of red fruit flavour and a stunning hot pink colour. And the best part of all? It's still just two ingredients, if you don't count the garnish.

Ingredients

- 60 mL (2 oz) Ruby Red grapefruit juice (fresh squeezed is best)
- 120 mL (4 oz) dry, sparkling Rosé
- Grapefruit slice (for garnish)

Instructions

- Pour the Ruby Red grapefruit juice into a sparkling wine flute. Hold the glass at a 45-degree angle and gently pour in the sparkling wine.
- Garnish with a grapefruit slice and enjoy!

French 100

The French 75 is another classic cocktail, and in true Sparkling Winos fashion, we've turned the dial from 75 up to 100!

We use cognac instead of gin and honey instead of simple syrup, and we top it with a French macaron because, well, it's so French and over the top. The added touch of the macaron makes it the perfect cocktail for an extra festive celebration (and yes, it's socially acceptable to eat the garnish).

Ingredients

- 45 mL (1.5 oz) cognac
- 22 mL (3/4 oz) lemon juice (about 3/4 of a lemon, juiced)
- 11 mL (3/4 tbsp) honey
- 90 mL (3 oz) dry sparkling wine
- French macaron (for garnish)

Instructions

- Fill a cocktail shaker with ice. Pour in the cognac, lemon juice and honey. Don't pour in the sparkling wine or you might be wearing the cocktail instead!
- Put on the lid and shake vigorously for 20 seconds until chilled and all the ingredients are combined. Strain the liquid into a sparkling wine flute, and top with sparkling wine.
- Garnish with a French macaron, embrace being extra, and enjoy!

Niagara Peach Bellini

Bellinis are a longstanding brunch staple, and a great alternative to their more popular cousin, the Mimosa. Though they require a bit more work than just simply pouring sparkling wine over juice, the effort with a Bellini is worth the payoff. We couldn't resist adding a little Canadian flair to this Italian classic, and the result is pretty peachy freakin' keen, if we do say so ourselves!

Ingredients

- 60 mL (2 oz) peach purée (about 1 ripe peach, peeled and blended) or peach nectar
- 120 mL (4 oz) dry sparkling wine (bonus points if it's Canadian)
- 15 mL (0.5 oz) Canadian Icewine
- Peach slice (for garnish)

Instructions

- To make the peach purée, simply peel a ripe peach and blend it in a blender or food processor until smooth. Chill it for at least 30 minutes afterwards for best results.
- Pour the peach purée or peach nectar into a sparkling wine flute. Hold the glass at a 45-degree angle and gently pour in the sparkling wine.
- Top with 0.5 oz Icewine (Vidal or Riesling works best in this case).
- Garnish with a peach slice and enjoy!

Sparkling Sangria Blanco

Everybody loves Sangria, so we decided to put a Sparkling Winos spin on it. And through our fair share of testing over the years, we think we have developed the perfect Sangria recipe. We call it the Sparkling Sangria Blanco.

Ingredients (yields one pitcher)

- 1 bottle of Cava (or other dry sparkling wine)
- 120 mL (4 oz) Brandy
- 60 mL (2 oz) orange liqueur (like Cointreau or Grand Marnier)
- 120 mL (4 oz) orange juice
- 1 cup fresh fruit, sliced (use whatever you have in the fridge, but we like lemon, orange, nectarine and, if you have it, white cranberry)
- Fresh mint (for garnish)

Instructions

- Fill a pitcher about halfway with ice. Add 1 cup fresh fruit, sliced.
- Add Brandy, orange liqueur and orange juice.
- Top with 1 bottle of Cava (or other dry sparkling wine).
- Stir gently, allow a few minutes to chill.
- Pour into a stemless wine glass, garnish with fresh mint and enjoy!

Chapter 7:

FROM GRAPE TO GLASS

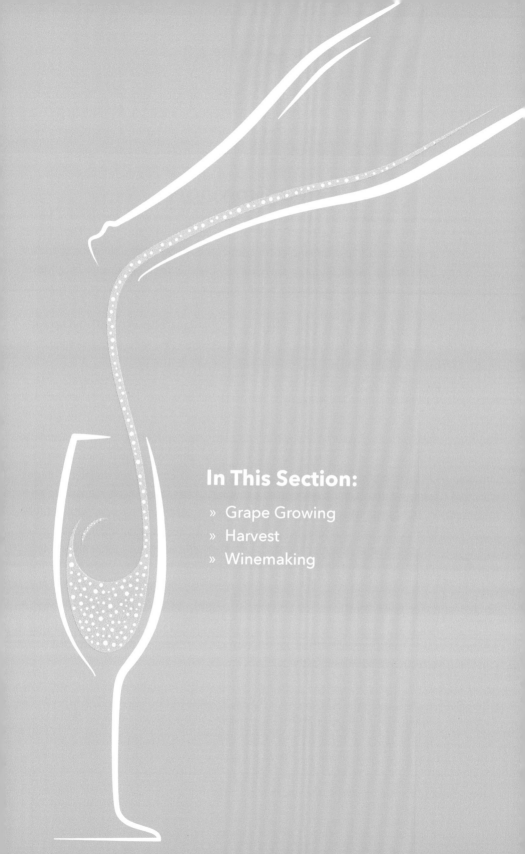

In This Section:

The Root of It All

Now that you know some of the sparkling wine ground rules, including how to taste, evaluate and pair it with food, as well as use it in cocktails, we think it's time to go back to the root of it all ... literally! In this chapter, we will talk about how sparkling wine is made, so let's start from the ground up.

Grape Growing

The ideal viticulture zone is between 30° - 50° latitude, both north and south. Though this is a relatively wide band when looking at the globe, the grapes best suited for sparkling wine come from cooler climate regions within this band, where they ripen at a slower pace and achieve lower sugar levels and higher acidity.

There are three key factors to consider when growing grapes: **climate**, **soil** and **terrain**. These three factors, in turn, come together to comprise a wine term that you may have heard: **terroir**. To put it simply, terroir is a wine's "sense of place."

Let's talk about the first factor: **climate**.

You may have also heard the terms "warm climate" and "cool climate" thrown around when discussing wine before, or perhaps you've seen them on a label or in marketing materials. As you can probably guess, warm climate wines come from warmer climates, and cool climate wines come from cooler climates. Pretty simple, eh? But what does that mean in the glass? Warm climate wines can be described as riper and rounder (fuller-bodied and smoother in texture), whereas cooler climate wines can be described as elegant, crisp and fresh. Sounds like the perfect set of descriptors for sparkling wine, right?

To get a feel for what we mean, try picking up a bottle of Chardonnay from a warm-climate region (like California) and one from a cool-climate region (like Chablis). You'll probably notice that the California Chardonnay is richer and concentrated, while the Chablis is restrained and mineral driven.

That example aside, we'd like to point out that many factors affect climate, including humidity, rainfall, and cooling or warming elements like wind patterns or cloud cover. These factors will also contribute to the heartiness of different grape varieties and their ability to thrive in a given climate. Grapes such as Riesling, Pinot Noir and Sauvignon Blanc prefer a slower, cooler ripening season, whereas grapes such as Zinfandel, Grenache, and Syrah do well in the warm sun.

While it's important to note that cool climate regions provide conditions for fruit well suited for sparkling wine, these regions are not without challenges. Extreme temperatures and the threat of frost can be devastating and can wipe out an entire harvest if they strike at the wrong time. But, as most cool-climate winemakers will tell you, the risk is worth the reward. Many use innovations like thermal blankets, weather monitoring and vine hilling to push for productive vines in challenging conditions. What can we say? It's a labour of love!

Soil is the second important factor.

Soil composition, that is – the combination of minerals, rocks and dirt – attributes a mineral character to the fruit and, in turn, the wine. This is obvious in places with limestone-rich soils like the Champagne region in France. The soil's surface can also help to reflect or absorb heat (depending upon its colour). Stones on the surface can heat up in the sun during the day, retaining some of that heat into the evening, protecting vines from the elements. Soil drainage is also important, as some grape varieties thrive in dry conditions, while others prefer a bit of extra moisture.

Terrain is the third factor.

The physical features of the vineyard have a profound impact on grape growing. Altitude – the height of land relative to sea level – will impact temperatures. Higher altitudes will result in cooler temperatures, allowing growers in warmer regions (like Argentina) to grow grapes suited for sparkling wine and still preserve their acidity. The aspect, or the direction that a slope faces, will help determine the amount of sunlight the vines will receive, impacting their productivity and ability to ripen. In addition, other geological features, such as large bodies of water, will also help to moderate temperature swings in vineyards. This is a critical and defining element in many cool-climate regions, like Franciacorta or Ontario. In these cases, surrounding bodies of water heat up in the summer and provide a warming effect over the cool winter months. Likewise, these large bodies of water cool down in the winter and provide a cooling effect over the hot summer months.

While the first step in crafting a quality sparkling wine starts with the careful tending of vines and grapes themselves, the second step is a successful harvest. Picking at the right time can make or break a wine. This is no truer than for grapes destined to become sparkling wine. Grapes intended for use in sparkling winemaking are harvested first, and will be slightly under-ripe, when the fruits' natural acidity is high, and its sugars are still relatively low (at approximately 17.5-18 *Brix*). This results in a base wine with bright fruit flavours, high acidity, and an Alcohol by Volume (ABV) of approximately 10 to 11% (an additional 1.5% occurs naturally during the secondary fermentation).

Some producers choose to harvest by hand, selecting only the finest fruit for this delicate style of wine. But harvesting by machine is also widespread. The grapes are usually picked in the early morning or late evening (when temperatures are lower) and quickly transported to the winemaking facility for pressing to avoid the premature fruit oxidation. Once we have the *must* (the pressed grape juice), it's time for the magic to happen!

Winemaking

As we mentioned at the beginning of this book, there are many ways to make sparkling wine. We will focus on the two most popular: the **Traditional Method** and the **Charmat Method**, which account for most of the world's sparkling wine production.

Both methods start similarly, but they diverge mid-way through the winemaking process. The critical difference is that Traditional Method sparkling wines undergo a secondary fermentation in the bottle, and Charmat Method sparkling wines undergo a secondary fermentation in a stainless-steel tank.

The Traditional Method

- **Step 1**: The grapes are harvested early to achieve lower sugar and higher acid levels, then sorted to ensure only the highest quality fruit is used.
- **Step 2**: Each grape variety is gently pressed to produce a clear juice.
- **Step 3**: These clear juices undergo a primary fermentation in stainless steel tanks or oak barrels, resulting in still, dry base wines.
- **Step 4**: The base wines are blended in different amounts (in a process called *assemblage*) to create the final blend (or cuvée), which may originate from multiple years for non-vintage wines or a single harvest for vintage (Millésimé) wines.
- **Step 5**: The blended wine is bottled, and a mixture of sugar and yeast is added to each bottle to ignite the secondary fermentation in the bottle (tirage). It is sealed with a crown cap (like that on a beer bottle). The bottles are placed on their sides in a cellar and the secondary fermentation occurs over a period of six to eight weeks. The CO_2 produced during the secondary fermentation (from the conversion of sugar to alcohol) remains trapped inside the liquid and … we've got bubbles!
- **Step 6**: The bottles rest *sur lie*, which means that they rest with the spent yeast cells inside each bottle. This adds complexity and structure (mainly the toasty/brioche notes associated with Traditional Method sparkling wines). The process lasts anywhere from nine months to several years, depending upon the quality and aging requirements where the wine is being produced.
- **Step 7**: The dead yeast cells are collected in the neck of the bottle (through a process called *riddling*). Traditionally, riddling was carried out by hand using a riddling rack, but nowadays, it's almost always automated for efficiency (though several high-end examples or smaller boutique operations still riddle by hand). During this process, the bottles are gradually rotated and inverted until all the dead yeast cells are collected in the neck of the bottle.
- **Step 8**: The dead yeast cells are then removed from the bottle (through a process called disgorgement). The neck of the bottle is placed in a bath of freezing brine, until the wine and lees are frozen. Then the cap on the bottle is removed, and the frozen sediment shoots right out in the form of an ice cube.
- **Step 9**: But now you're left with a bottle missing a couple of inches of wine! This is where the dosage comes in. The dosage is a mixture of still wine and sugar that is quickly added after the sediment is disgorged and before the cork is put in place. The added sugar determines the final sweetness of the wine (such as Brut Nature, Brut or Demi-Sec.)
- **Step 10**: The cork is put in place, the bottles run through a high-tech labelling machine, and voila! Before being shipped off for sale, most Traditional Method sparkling wines will rest for an additional six months or so to ensure the dosage is fully integrated.

Step 1
Harvest

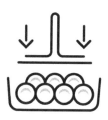

Step 2
Pressing

Step 3
Primary Fermentation

Step 4
Blending

Step 5
Secondary Fermentation

Step 6
Aging

Step 7
Riddling

Step 8
Disgorgement

Step 9
Dosage

Step 10
Corking & Labelling

Step 1
Harvest

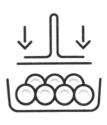

Step 2
Pressing

Step 3
Primary Fermentation

Step 4
Secondary Fermentation

Step 5
Filtration

Step 6
Dosage

Step 7
Bottling

Step 8
Corking & Labelling

The Charmat Method

- **Step 1**: The grapes are harvested early to achieve lower sugar and higher acid levels, then sorted to ensure only the highest quality fruit is used.
- **Step 2**: The grapes are gently pressed to produce a clear juice.
- **Step 3**: This clear juice undergoes a primary fermentation (usually in stainless steel tanks), resulting in a still, dry base wine. The base wine may be from a single variety or it may be an assemblage.
- **Step 4**: The base wine is transferred to sealed and pressurized stainless-steel tanks (called autoclaves) where a mixture of sugar and yeast is added to begin the secondary fermentation, which occurs over a period of up to six weeks. Since these tanks are sealed and pressurized, the CO_2 produced during the fermentation (from the conversion of sugar to alcohol) cannot escape and remains trapped in the wine.
- **Step 5**: Once the secondary fermentation is complete, the wine is filtered under pressure and transferred to another tank to remove the lees.
- **Step 6**: A dosage is added to the tank to bring the wine to its desired sweetness level.
- **Step 7**: Then the wine is bottled – still under the same amount of pressure as it was in the tank – using a special bottling machine.
- **Step 8**: The bottles run through a high-tech labelling machine, and voila!

Pop the Bubbly, You've Just Graduated Sparkling Wine 101

Congratulations! Now that you're armed with everything you need to know about crafting, tasting, pairing, evaluating, and enjoying sparkling wine - dig out your passports, because we're about to take you on a journey around the world. We'll visit all our favourite sparkling wine regions, demystifying the key sparkling wine styles from each. We'll show-and-tell some of our favourite stories and snapshots from our travels. So, pack your bags, and hopefully we'll inspire you to return home with a few new bottles to try!

Chapter 8:

FRANCE

Champagne caves 03/2019

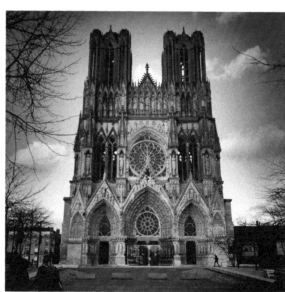

Reims Cathedral

France: An Introduction

France, home to Champagne and a variety of regionally produced Crémant, is a powerhouse of quality sparkling wine production. We have the French to thank for honing not only the art of sparkling winemaking, but the art of marketing it as well. Rarely does a birthday, graduation, holiday gathering or other celebration go by without hearing the expression: "Pop the Champagne!"

Champagne is one of, if not the most famous wine regions in the world. Its roots are firmly planted in northeastern France's cool, somewhat unforgiving climate. This cool climate helps growers and winemakers produce a distinctive, often-emulated-but-never-duplicated style of wine. Despite global competitors champing at the bit – creating easy-drinking, approachable sparkling wines or applying a carbon copy formula in an effort to recreate it – Champagne continues to set the gold standard.

But it's not just Champagne that sets France apart in the sparkling department. Crémant, produced across the country, offers up a whole other dimension of effervescence for bubbleheads to explore.

The Champagne and the various Crémant-producing regions are all governed by the *Appellation d'Origine Contrôlée (AOC)*, which translates to the "Controlled Designation of Origin." An AOC certifies a product's authenticity and, in the case of wine, the *appellation* sets specific standards and requirements that producers and winemakers must follow or fulfill. These requirements vary between the Champagne and the various Crémant-producing AOCs, but they generally set minimum requirements that, across the board, guarantee sparkling wine is made in the Traditional Method. You won't find Charmat Method wines in any of these AOCs.

So, let's explore!

CHAMPAGNE

Grape Varieties
Chardonnay, Pinot
Noir & Pinot Meunier

Production Method
Traditional

Price Point
$$$

Primary Aromas & Flavours

- Citrus
- Brioche
- Yellow Apple
- Almond
- Minerality

Sweetness

Dry   Sweet

Body

Light-Bodied   Full-Bodied

Acidity

Low   High

Alcohol

Low   High

Serving Temperature
7 - 10°C

Glassware
White Wine or Tulip Glass

Cellaring Potential
3 - 10 Years

Sparkling Spotlight: Champagne

The name Champagne suggests joy, exuberance and festivity. It's no surprise – it has been marketed as the wine of celebration for what seems like hundreds of years now.

Geography

The Champagne AOC, located in northeastern France about 150 kilometres east of Paris, is the defined area from which Champagne can originate. Initially identified in the late 1920s, the production zone now encompasses approximately 34,000 hectares (about 84,700 acres) of vineyards. These are further divided into a complex web of approximately 289,000 privately held plots. Having visited several producers and their plots, we can attest how managing these (and their owners) can be a business unto itself!

Interestingly, the Champagne AOC is not contiguous and is divided into four main growing areas: Montagne de Reims, Vallée de la Marne, Côte des Blancs and Côte des Bar (which includes the exclave of Aube). In addition, there are several other smaller sub-areas, including Massif de Saint-Thierry, Vallée de L'Ardre, Côte de Sézanne and Montgueux.

While distinct from one another, two principal centres anchor these sub-regions: the beautiful and historic hilltop city of Reims and the charming town of Épernay, home to the Avenue de Champagne. Peppered throughout the region are hundreds of small villages, 17 of which have a traditional entitlement to "Grand Cru" ranking and 42 to "Premier Cru." While great for marketing, this classification does not have any further, formal meaning today.

Each of the major sub-regions also showcases unique strengths and specializations (which may include a focal grape variety, such as Pinot Meunier in the Vallée de la Marne or Chardonnay in the Côte des Blancs). The sub-regions may also specialize in the production of a particular expression of Champagne, such as Blanc de Noirs or Blanc de Blancs.

Fizz Fact:

"Come quickly, I am tasting the stars."

You've probably seen this quote somewhere adjacent to sparkling wine, right?

Contrary to popular belief, Dom Pérignon – the famous, or infamous, monk from l'Abbaye Saint-Pierre in Hautvillers – did not utter those words, nor did he invent the wine we now call Champagne.

Born in the 1600s, his physical presence predated sparkling wine becoming the dominant style in the region by over one hundred years. His research centred mostly on stopping in-bottle refermentation (which is the process through which sparkling wine gets, well, its sparkle). During his lifetime, refermentation was literally causing explosions in the cellar and giving winemakers significant heartache. Dom Pérignon made several observations and recommendations that many winemakers would apply, such as blending a cuvée from several vineyards and harvesting on cool mornings.

It's not all myth and marketing though.

The abbey where Dom Pérignon lived was part of a long monastic presence in the Champagne region that was directly linked to wine: it was responsible for maintaining viticultural practices brought to the Champagne region by the Romans. They knew to plant on hillside slopes with good drainage and with maximum sunlight exposure to support the ripening of grapes for wine (sounds like Winegrowing 101, eh?). You could say they were the earliest connoisseurs of Champagne, though it is tough to say if the wines of that day exhibited any accidental effervescence.

Sparkling Spotlight:

Benoît Tarlant
Proprietor, Grower & Winemaker
Champagne Tarlant

We asked Benoît, "What makes Champagne so special?"

"Of course, we could say it is its location, vines and weather, which are very particular. But, Champagne is nothing without its people – the women and men of the Champagne region – who continue to take care of this very civilized plant, that is the vine. The Champenois have carefully worked their vineyards, which bore grapes that became bubbly wine, by chance, hard work and abnegation, in this, not so peaceful area.

"We are lucky, my sister and I, to be the part of the Tarlant family, being winegrowers in Champagne since 1687, and we are proud of our past, but we are also responsible for its future. We are making Champagne in keeping with tradition, but we also look to modernity."

Production

Champagne is a Traditional Method wine. The perfection of this production method is closely tied to the region, resulting in one of the Traditional Method's global names: the "Méthode Champenoise." Successful lobbying by the *Comité interprofessionnel du vin de Champagne (CIVC)* and the European Union has resulted in Champagne being designated a protected term in most countries.

The principal grapes in the production of Champagne are Chardonnay, Pinot Noir and Pinot Meunier (sometimes simply called Meunier). As some would say, this trio produces the perfect cuvée.

What does each bring to the blend?

Chardonnay – a white grape variety – is relatively easy to grow in the chalky soils of the region and brings backbone and aging potential to the blend. Pinot Noir – a red grape variety – is also well suited to the cool climate of the Champagne region and it brings body and complexity. Rounding out the trio is Pinot Meunier – another red grape variety – which brings roundness and a fruity character to the cuvée. In the case of the two Pinots, they are pressed gently with limited or no skin contact, producing white juice. Rosé Champagne is produced through skin contact with the juice (also known as the Rosé Saignée method) or by adding a dosage of red wine.

These three cool kids aren't alone in keeping the Champagne show running. While Chardonnay, Pinot Noir and Pinot Meunier account for approximately 30%, 38% and 32% of plantings, approximately 0.3% are comprised of the other approved grape varieties of the Champagne AOC: Pinot Blanc, Pinot Gris, Arbane and Petit Meslier. Some producers, such as Tarlant, are revisiting the whole gamut of permitted varieties and producing wines from these lesser-known varieties.

The economy of Champagne is serious business. According to the CIVC, in 2021, it comprised 16,200 winegrowers, 360 *Maisons* (or houses), 130 co-operatives, a productive area of nearly 34,000 hectares (as previously mentioned), and almost 245 million bottles of Champagne. Those 245 million bottles had a value of €4.2 billion in 2021, of which approximately €2.3 billion was from exports. It's fair to say that the French love their Champagne (and we don't blame them).

Are you worried about a global Champagne shortage? Don't be. In addition to all those exports, producers also have a stockpile of over 1 billion bottles stashed away as reserve wines for blending, future sales and, perhaps, rainy days. Hey, there are a lot of those in Champagne!

Very rarely do Maisons own all their vineyards. You're probably wondering: so how do they produce their wines?

There are more than 16,200 growers in Champagne and they collectively own approximately 90% of the vineyards in the region.

Among these growers are about 5,000 that produce what are called *Grower Champagnes*. Sound familiar? Grower Champagnes – or Les Champagnes de Vignerons – are wines produced by growers and grower-cooperatives in a way that reflects and respects local terroir and vineyard sites. These wines showcase unique qualities. In some ways, they are the antithesis of the almost-always-identical house style of the *Grandes Marques*.

And speaking of producers in the region, they are identified on the label with specific abbreviations to give you a sense of the provenance of the finished product you are enjoying:

- **Négociant manipulant (NM)**: Indicates that this firm bought grapes, wine must or wine to make Champagne (this includes all the Grandes Marques).

- **Récoltant manipulant (RM)**: Indicates that this firm is a grower and makes and markets Champagne from grapes originating from their own vineyards.

- **Récoltant-coopérateur (RC)**: Indicates a cooperative grower selling Champagne produced by a cooperative, under their own label.

- **Coopérative de manipulation (CM)**: Indicates a cooperative that makes Champagne from members' grapes, which were collectively used.

- **Société de Récoltants (SR)**: Indicates a family firm of growers making and marketing a Champagne under its own label (but who are not a cooperative enterprise).

- **Négociant distributeur (ND)**: Indicates a wine merchant or distributor selling finished bottles of Champagne under its own label.

- **Marque auxiliaire** or **Marque d'Acheteur (MA)**: Indicates a private label made for a client (e.g., a supermarket chain or celebrity – such as a famous and now-divorced couple who not only made wines in Provence but also recently expanded to Champagne – under a custom label).

Fizz Fact:

Champagne is noted for its minerality, imparted to the wine by the chalky soils that predominate in the region. But winemakers - or schoolteachers in search of writing materials - were not the first to notice this whitish substance.

The earth below the historic city of Reims - with its stunning cathedral and plethora of Champagne houses, both large and small - has been mined since times immemorial. The Gauls, Romans and Normans, along with the medieval and modern-day French of course, mined the hilltop because chalk was a cheap building material. It's not the most resilient substance so few, if any, structures made of chalk survive to this day. But these early industrial efforts did leave behind nearly 200 kilometres of chalk tunnels.

And what, you may be wondering, does chalk have to do with Champagne?

In the middle of the 18th century, Nicolas Ruinart converted an abandoned chalk quarry into a cellar for his wine, discovering that the cool, damp, dark, ambient, and stable conditions were perfect for the storing and aging of sparkling wine. The rest, they say, is history as many houses followed suit, snapping up plots of land with chalk tunnels. Veuve Clicquot, Taittinger, GH Mumm, Pommery, Charles Heidsieck and, indeed, Ruinart all have chalk cellars (some of which, thankfully, are open to visitors).

Sparkling Spotlight:

Olivier Krug
Director of the House
Krug Champagne

We asked Olivier, "What makes Champagne so special?"

"What makes Champagne so special is the fact that it is always connected to our best life moments and pleasure. This is why my second great grandfather, Joseph Krug, dreamt of creating a Champagne that would aim for the very best quality every year, as well as offering the most generous expression of Champagne in one glass. I personally love to perpetuate his vision, dedicating my own life connecting with Krug Lovers, all around the world. I, myself, will not forget Jeff and Mike's emotion when we first met at Krug, for a journey through different creations of Krug that we specifically paired with music."

Profile & Characteristics

How does one define Champagne's profile and characteristics in a mere paragraph or two? A tall order, we think, but we will do our best.

As a wine made in the Traditional Method, Champagne will be complex and rich. It will balance fruitiness with secondary and tertiary characteristics, such as minerality, toast, honey, and nuts. A Brut, house style from a Grande Marque – meant to be enjoyed in any setting – will likely be your gateway to the category. Such a style will typically be fruit-forward, with touches of what many consider the other hallmarks of Champagne: chalky minerality and *autolysis* (imparting a bready, yeasty character).

A Blanc de Noirs Champagne, made from Pinot Noir, Pinot Meunier or a blend of both, sees no or little skin contact meaning the wine will be white, perhaps with a rose-gold hue. Wines made in this style will often showcase greater body and a red fruit and berry character.

A Blanc de Blancs Champagne, made from Chardonnay (or a blend including the significantly rarer Pinot Gris, Pinot Blanc, Arbane, or Petit Meslier) will express not only crisp white tree fruit and citrus, but also minerality and acidity.

We have spent many an evening debating whether we prefer Blanc de Noirs or Blanc de Blancs and have not reached a polite consensus. When the needle moves one way, we try another example and … oops, we're back to loving a tried, tested, and true cuvée made from the classic trio. Go figure!

Ultimately, though, whether classic Brut, or Blanc de Noirs or Blancs, there are many factors influencing the profile of a Champagne, including area or sub-region of origin, winemaking and winemaker choices (like extended lees aging, dosage and level of residual sugar), and disgorgement date.

Whatever the factors, we say the best way to experience Champagne, and any sparkling wine, is to taste it yourself, as the experience is intensely personal!

Fizz Fact:

Sorry Avenue des Champs-Élysées, we don't think you are the most beautiful street in the world. While this Parisian drag may be the world's most famous, we feel the honour belongs to Épernay's Avenue de Champagne. But hey, we're the Sparkling Winos, after all.

Running for over a kilometre through the historic centre of Épernay, the Avenue de Champagne is lined with the front lawns, driveways, gates and facades of buildings associated with – you guessed it – Champagne houses. Some of these buildings were built as headquarters for Grandes Marques and grower-producers, and others were built as the private houses of owners or as warehouses (some with chalk cellars, to boot). In any case, the architectural style of the streetscape of the region's most iconic street is eclectic and monumental, and the whole ensemble certainly makes an impression!

We had the pleasure of tasting at Moët & Chandon, located on a prestigious site on the Avenue de Champagne, in a charming historic villa said to have been visited by Napoleon himself. We don't care too much for megalomaniacs, and the region sure does love its mythology, so the facts can sometimes be hard to verify! But we can declare with absolute empirical certainty that we did enjoy a vertical tasting of several vintages of Champagne. So all in all, it was a successful day in Napoleon's Imperial Salon.

Sparkling Spotlight:

Nicolas Rainon
Proprietor, Grower & Geologist

Champagne Henriet-Bazin

We asked Nicolas, "What makes Champagne so special?"

"As a Champagne grower, I do my best to ensure that each bunch of grapes bears the taste of the plots of land from which it comes. Nature is my best ally to achieve this. I simply have to take care of the vines, treat each plot as I would like to be treated – with care, respect and attention, and as a partner, not as a supplier. For her part, Marie-Noëlle, my wife and the winemaker, blends this diverse mosaic of grape varieties, aromas of the soil or subsoil, balancing orientation and climatic singularity of each vintage, into cuvées that tell a chapter of the Henriet-Bazin story. But at the end of the day, it's only you who decides if this story is special."

CRÉMANT

Grape Varieties
Varies by Region

Production Method
Traditional

Price Point
$$

Primary Aromas & Flavours
- Citrus
- Cream
- Peach
- White Cherry
- Almond

Sweetness

Dry   Sweet

Body

Light-Bodied   Full-Bodied

Acidity

Low   High

Alcohol

Low   High

Serving Temperature
6 - 8°C

Glassware
White Wine or Tulip Glass

Cellaring Potential
1 - 3 Years

Sparkling Spotlight: Cremant

Crémant refers to a category of French sparkling wine. Meaning "creamy," the term originally referred to a less effervescent style of sparkling wine, bottled with fewer atmospheres of pressure than Champagne. Today, however, it refers to a Traditional Method sparkling wine produced in certain French AOCs, but outside Champagne.

What is so special about this sparkling wine style?

Plenty, to be honest.

Like Champagne, Crémant will represent a labour of love: the wine will be made in the Traditional Method and will rest on its lees for a defined amount of time. The length of time on lees varies across appellations but is typically a minimum of nine months (though some AOCs require 12 months). Crémant is intended to be enjoyed young.

Among the AOCs themselves, various grapes are permitted and are used to make Crémant. For bubbleheads like us, there is joy in exploring sparkling wine made from less common grape varieties, and beyond what would typically be used in Champagne (which continues to set the gold standard across the globe). While there are many technical reasons why Chardonnay, Pinot Noir and Pinot Meunier are the base of the Champagne blend, there's something exciting about a sparkling wine that reflects local tastes, viticultural history and, since this is France, appellation-based parameters.

Geography

You could say that Crémant is a regional sparkling wine.

Eight regions in France permit its production. They are Alsace, Bordeaux, Bourgogne (Burgundy), Die, Jura, Limoux, Loire and Savoie, the new kid on the block.

So, you're probably wondering: is Crémant from each region different? In short: yes!

Each region has a unique history, climate and viticultural context, and is governed by general and region-specific regulations, including permitted grapes.

Let's explore the eight regions.

Alsace

The region, located to the east of Champagne, exists in an agricultural and historical continuum with nearby Germany, so let's just say the Crémant produced there has a bit of a German accent. We won't wade into a tumultuous history of border re-drawing.

Crémant d'Alsace has been produced since the 1900s and is usually made from Pinot Blanc, though Riesling, Pinot Gris, Pinot Noir, Auxerrois and Chardonnay are also permitted. Rosé Crémant d'Alsace is also available and it is made from Pinot Noir. The grape varieties in the region reflect that, like the Champagne region, Alsace is a cool-climate viticultural region. Both white and Rosé Crémant d'Alsace will tend to be fresh, fruit-driven and elegant.

The region is no small producer: over 500 wineries produce Crémant d'Alsace, representing the most significant sparkling output among the approved Crémant appellations.

Bordeaux

Crémant de Bordeaux is a relatively new addition to this iconic French region, officially joining the ranks in 1990 (though sparkling wine has been produced here for over 100 years). Production has ramped up in the last 30 or so years, but despite the upswing, it represents only a tiny fraction of total output from the region's 500 or so vineyards. As a result, you're less likely to see these sparklers in the market.

So, what can you expect from a bottle of Crémant de Bordeaux?

Both red and white Bordeaux wines are blends, and there are a range of grapes permitted by the AOC, including Cabernet Sauvignon, Cabernet Franc, Merlot, Petit Verdot, Sauvignon Blanc, Ugni Blanc (Trebbiano) and Semillon. Most, if not all, varieties make it into Crémant de Bordeaux.

Bourgogne

Crémant de Bourgogne has a storied and celebrated history in Burgundy, dating back to the 1800s, with French poets writing about it enthusiastically. Things get a lot less romantic in the modern details: as with some other AOCs, Crémant de Bourgogne had its regulations formalized in the 1970s.

Chardonnay and Pinot Noir, the two Burgundian varieties, are naturally the base for sparkling wine here. Secondary varieties used for blending include Gamay, Aligoté, Melon, and Sacy. Mais oui!

The production of Crémant de Bourgogne is – surprise, surprise – subject to a variety of meticulous rules. For example, under-performing Pinot Noir during a poor growing season cannot simply be relegated for bubbles at a grower's behest. Rather, vineyards dedicated to Crémant de Bourgogne must be declared in spring. And it doesn't end there: harvesting protocols mimic the strictness of the Champagne region.

Crémant de Bourgogne is meant to be enjoyed young and the wines will have a youthful, fruit-forward profile. In an effort to boost quality and prestige though, the AOC introduced the Eminent and Grand Eminent denominations in 2013, which require a minimum aging time of 24 and 36 months, respectively. Wines made in these denominations will be richer, more complex and will possess more tertiary character on the nose and palate.

Die

We know: you're die-ing to know about Crémant de Die, right? Sorry, we love a good wine pun.

The region – officially welcomed into the fold with its own appellation in the mid-1990s – sits east of the Rhône River, just down from the Alps.

The bubbles here are made principally from the Clairette variety and Muscat and Aligoté. The wines tend to be dry and easy-drinking, with fruity and floral characters. Overall production is relatively small, at just over 200,000 bottles annually.

Oh, and let's be clairette, er, clear: Crémant de Die, while made from the Clairette grape, is not Clairette de Die. The latter (which also comes from the Rhône) is bottled before the first fermentation is complete and tends to have a kiss of sweetness.

According to local lore, this method of winemaking comes from Gallic tribes that would bury bottles by the Rhône River to keep them cool and temperature controlled. Forgotten for some time, these same bottles were later unearthed and supposedly revealed their bubbles to the lucky finder.

We think it's fair to say that it's not just Champagne that loves its mythology!

Jura

We're sure Jura interested in this Crémant, right? Sorry, another bad wine pun.

Jura is located between Burgundy and Switzerland, and as you'd expect from a mountainous area, it's a semi-continental and cool-climate wine region. Like Champagne, it's home to chalky soils that impart a distinct minerality to the wines made here.

The Crémant de Jura AOC dates to the 1990s and makes up only a small portion of the region's total output. (The area is known for its Vin Jaune – a sherry-like, yellow wine). Like some of its Crémant cousins, Crémant de Jura wines are less common and are made from Chardonnay, picked early and generally under-ripe to preserve acidity. Other permitted varieties for blending purposes include Pinot Noir, Trousseau, Poulsard and Savagnin.

Limoux

The Crémant de Limoux appellation has relatively modern origins in the 1990s, when more attention was given to the production of sparkling wine in the Languedoc region (which is known for its bulk wine). On the sparkling front, the region was historically known for its Blanquette de Limoux, an ancient sparkling wine made from Mauzac, an aromatic white grape. Supposedly, it predates Champagne and the wines of Die, and there are plenty of myths here to explore (that we'll put a pin in).

While Blanquette de Limoux may be Mauzac, err music, to a sparkling lover's ears, the Mauzac grape does not feature prominently in Crémant de Limoux. It is made primarily from Chardonnay and Chenin, with Mauzac and Pinot Noir permitted for blending purposes. Overall, the wine style is aromatic, fruit-forward and approachable.

As with all things in the highly productive Languedoc, output of Crémant de Limoux is not small: almost 6 million bottles are produced annually.

Loire

Famous for its beautiful chateaux, scenic river valley views and a maritime climate that includes temperamental, salty sea breezes, the Loire is also known for its use of Chenin. As in Crémant de Limoux, Crémant de Loire can be made with this grape variety, and some say, this is where it shines (though South Africa likely has an opinion about that). But Chenin is not slugging it alone in the production of sparkling in this region, as Chardonnay, Pinot Noir, Cabernet Franc, and a smattering of less familiar grape varieties make an appearance. From this assortment, you may be surprised to know that the second most common grape is Cabernet Franc, which is used to produce Blanc de Noirs and Rosé Crémant de Loire.

You could say that the Loire sparkles in more ways than one.

Though not a Crémant appellation, the region is also known for the production of Vouvray – a sparkling wine made in the Touraine area from the Chenin grape – and Saumur Mousseux AC – a sparkling wine that can be made from a blend of Chenin, Cabernet Franc and Chardonnay.

Savoie

And, last but not least, we have Savoie.

Recognized in 2015, Crémant de Savoie may be new, but sparkling production here has a long history.

With geography defined by steep slopes and vineyards occupying various altitudes, you could say things are alpine in this region. When tasting Crémant de Savoie, you will have a wine made most often from the aromatic Jacquère and Altesse grapes in your glass. Rounding out these two native grapes are Chasselas, Chardonnay, Pinot Noir and Gamay, with regulated proportions of each permitted dependent on the base wine's overall composition.

Crémant de Savoie will have a definite minerality and a fresh, floral character that makes it distinct from its sparkling peers.

Sparkling Reflections: France

In 2019, we had the pleasure of visiting the Champagne region for the second time. The trip was equal parts educational and exuberant (in every possible way), and we tasted our way through Maisons both large and small. We were humbled that so many incredible producers opened their doors for us.

We often reflect on this trip, which was nothing short of spiritual (though it was also incredibly demanding given how many tasting appointments we had arranged over two days). During this media trip, we did experience a peak Sparkling Winos moment: meeting the legendary Olivier Krug at iconic producer Krug.

We are lovers of Krug through and through, and it was such an honour to visit. We pinched ourselves as we tasted at the beautiful facility, observed hand-riddling, and saw firsthand how music can enhance the profile of Krug's incredible wines. It's fair to say that from the story of the Maison, to their attention to detail in the assemblage of the cuvée, to their incredible mystique – Krug is in a league of its own!

We don't think we've topped the Krug tasting experience … yet! – Mike

Chapter 9:

ITALY

Villa Barberina 08/2016

Picking figs with Primo Franco

Italy: An Introduction

Italy holds its own as one of the world's greatest sparkling wine producers. Given its geography and climate, it's no surprise that northern Italy is the heartland of Italian bubbly. It is home to five distinct sparkling-wine-producing regions and wine styles: Prosecco, Franciacorta, Trento, Asti and Lambrusco.

In each of these five regions, sparkling wines are produced in accordance with the regulations within a respective Indicazione Geografica Tipica (IGT), *Denominazione di Origine Controllata (DOC)* or Denominazione di Origine Controllata e Garantita (DOCG) designation. Each will have its own standards and defined area, with the most stringent regulations found in a DOCG.

But let's get back to the bubbles!

Prosecco has surged in popularity, so much so that for many casual bubbleheads, the name Prosecco is synonymous with sparkling wine. "I'll have a glass of Prosecco," can be heard in bars across the world. And while Prosecco may be at the forefront of Italy's sparkling wines in terms of consumer popularity, approachability, and growing market dominance, as we've discovered through Sparkling Winos, there is much more to Italian sparkling wine!

Italy's bubbles are as unique and diverse as its world-famous cuisine. In addition to fruit-dominant Charmat Method wines from Prosecco and Asti, the country also offers rich and complex Traditional Method wines from Franciacorta and Trento, along with sparkling reds – that is, Lambrusco.

PROSECCO

Grape Varieties
Glera

Production Method
Charmat

Price Point
$

Primary Aromas & Flavours

- Green Apple
- Pear
- Peach
- Honeysuckle
- Cream

Sweetness

Dry   Sweet

Body

Light-Bodied   Full-Bodied

Acidity

Low   High

Alcohol

Low   High

Serving Temperature
4 - 7°C

Glassware
Flute or Tulip Glass

Cellaring Potential
None

Sparkling Spotlight: Prosecco

The rise in Prosecco's popularity over the past few years has been astronomical – you've probably tasted this wine style at least once or twice. It now outsells Champagne worldwide, and several years ago, producers sparked concerns of a global shortage!

Geography

Prosecco is made in a large area spanning several provinces in the Veneto and Friuli Venezia Giulia regions of northeastern Italy, in the Prosecco DOC appellation (located in proximity to the historic city of Venice).

Carved out of this large area are two additional DOCs – Prosecco Treviso and Prosecco Trieste – and two DOCGs – Prosecco Conegliano Valdobbiadene Superiore and Asolo Prosecco Superiore. Each corresponds to a surrounding town or area and includes a smaller growing area. In the case of the DOCGs, there are additional regulations than otherwise found within the larger Prosecco DOC.

But it does not end there: to recognize unique microclimates within the Prosecco Conegliano Valdobbiadene Superiore DOCG, the Hill of Cartizze and over 40 sub-zones along the River Piave have been identified.

Production

Prosecco is made principally from the Glera grape, a white wine grape known for its neutral profile. A minimum of 85% Glera must be used, with other permitted varieties including Chardonnay, Pinot Noir, Pinot Blanc and a selection of indigenous grapes.

Prosecco is produced in the Charmat Method, or commonly referred to in Italian, the "Metodo Martinotti" or "Metodo Italiano."

Why the different names? Well, this production method was developed and patented by an Italian œnologist named Federico Martinotti in the 1890s but further refined and popularized by French inventor Eugène Charmat a few decades later. Through Eugène may get all the glory in the English-speaking wine world, Italians tend to emphasize their native son when talking about the method in which Prosecco, and other wines, are made.

Speaking of which, we're sure Federico would be pleased to hear that annual production hovers around 486 million bottles.

Sparkling Spotlight:

Sandro Bottega
President & CEO

Bottega SpA

We asked Sandro, "What makes Prosecco so special?"

"Prosecco is a sparkling wine of great tradition, combining freshness and aromatic complexity. Its fruity (golden apples, pears, peaches, citrus fruits) and floral (acacia, wisteria, lily of the valley) scents satisfy the palate of connoisseurs and newcomers to the world of wine. Its great versatility makes it a wine for the whole meal, which lends itself to a variety of food combinations, ranging from aperitifs to desserts.

"Bottega Gold, the Prosecco DOC characterized by its golden bottle, originates from grapes of excellence from the hilly area of Valdobbiadene, the heart of the territory awarded UNESCO World Heritage status. This wine is one of the highest expressions of the Bottega winery, based in Bibano di Godega, 50 kilometres north of Venice. For many years now, the company has made an unbreakable commitment to sustainability, leading to real, concrete results in reducing its impact on the environment, society and the economy."

Profile & Characteristics

So, what can you expect from Prosecco?

As it is made principally from one main grape variety – Glera – and produced in the Charmat Method, you will experience a light-bodied, vibrant, fresh, highly aromatic, easy-drinking style of sparkling wine with medium to high acidity and larger bubbles. Dominant flavours include apple, honeysuckle, peach, melon, and pear.

Prosecco Rosé, which was permitted to be labelled as of 2020 and hit the shelves in 2021, is made from a blend of Glera and Pinot Noir and offers up plenty of fresh red berry fruit on the nose and palate. The addition of Pinot Noir adds body and structure to Prosecco Rosé, in comparison to Prosecco. Previously, Prosecco Rosé was simply labelled *Spumante*.

When it comes to the level of sweetness, if you prefer your Prosecco dry, make sure to reach for a bottle with Brut on the label. Brut Prosecco and Brut Prosecco Rosé will contain less than 12 grams of residual sugar per litre. Somewhat counterintuitively, wines labelled Extra Dry and Dry Prosecco will contain more sugar than Brut Prosecco (12-17 and 17-32 grams per litre, respectively).

This wine style is delicious on its own as an aperitif, and it pairs effortlessly with lighter and heavier fare, including chips, charcuterie, polenta, and fried seafood. It's also fantastic in a cocktail, such as the ever-popular Aperol Spritz, the classic Bellini or the ubiquitous Mimosa.

Aside from being a vibrant, fruit-forward wine style, Prosecco is also typically available at an affordable price compared to many other sparkling styles, making it an approachable, everyday wine that need not be reserved for special occasions. For these reasons, and undoubtedly for many more, Prosecco is one of the most popular sparkling wines in the world.

Fizz Fact:

The steep and incredibly scenic hill of Cartizze has long been considered the most prized location to produce premium Prosecco. Superiore di Cartizze is known for its pronounced fruity character and kiss of sweetness. We had the pleasure of visiting Col Vetoraz, which sits atop Cartizze. We tasted its namesake wines while taking in the sweeping views - and we highly recommend visiting and tasting the "Grand Cru" of Prosecco!

Sparkling Spotlight:

Silvia Franco
Proprietor
Nino Franco

We asked Silvia, "What makes Prosecco so special?"

"Prosecco is so special for several reasons! First of all, the territory of Conegliano Valdobbiadene DOCG is a very special place, providing perfect soil and landscape for the growth of the Glera grape. These hills were recognized as a UNESCO World Heritage Site in 2019. Prosecco shows a unique expression of the Italian lifestyle: it is a cheerful sparkling wine, to toast every single day, with friends or simply alone. It is for any occasion, not just the 'special' ones. Prosecco gathers people joyfully and puts a smile on their faces!"

FRANCIACORTA

Grape Varieties
Chardonnay, Pinot
Noir & Pinot Blanc

Production Method
Traditional

Price Point
$$$

Primary Aromas & Flavours
- Citrus
- Peach
- Toast
- Almond
- Minerality

Sweetness

Dry   Sweet

Body

Light-Bodied   Full-Bodied

Acidity

Low   High

Alcohol

Low   High

Serving Temperature
7 - 10°C

Glassware
White Wine or Tulip Glass

Cellaring Potential
3 - 6 Years

Sparkling Spotlight: Franciacorta

Some call Franciacorta the "Champagne of Italy." While we are not fans of the term "Champagne of [insert any other region]" because Champagne cannot be replicated (though it can be emulated), there is plenty to be said about Franciacorta in its own right.

Geography

Franciacorta is made in the Italian region of Lombardy. Though winemaking in the region has a long history, the modern Franciacorta DOC originated in the 1960s. Since the mid-1990s, sparkling wines from the region have been made under the Franciacorta DOCG (and still wines hailing from the region can be produced and labelled under other, differently named appellations).

Franciacorta is a compact wine region: the DOCG comprises just under 20 Italian communes clustered south of Lake Iseo – which offers a moderating effect on nearby vineyards – and north of the city of Brescia.

Production

Chardonnay, Pinot Noir and Pinot Blanc are the permitted grape varieties in the Franciacorta DOCG. The wines are made exclusively in the "Metodo Classico" (Traditional Method), and labelling standards are like those in the Champagne region.

Minimum times apply for aging sur lie: 18 months for non-vintage Brut, 24 months for non-vintage Brut Rosé, 30 months for vintage Franciacorta, and 60 months for riserva wines.

You may also see the label Satèn, which denotes a Blanc de Blancs Franciacorta, aged at least 24 months sur lie and subject to less atmospheric pressure in bottle. It lives up to its name – silky. Apropos, considering one of the world's fashion capitals, Milan, is just a stone's throw away (and the region has a history of producing silk).

Within the Franciacorta DOCG, there is a vineyard area of approximately 2,900 hectares (7,160 acres). About 15.6 million bottles are produced annually, and only 10% is exported. It's fair to say that Italians are keeping Franciacorta close to their hearts (and in their glasses).

When examining the production method, principal grapes and labelling conventions used in the making of Franciacorta, we can see some parallels with Champagne. But when zeroing in, we can see that the wines are made in a slightly warmer region so they will have less acidity and show a more fruity character.

Profile and Character

We are often asked: how different are Franciacorta and Prosecco?

Night and day may be a bit extreme, but there is a significant difference between these two wine styles. Given the production method, Franciacorta will typically be much richer in profile and character than Prosecco, with a more delicate *perlage* that can't be achieved using the Charmat Method. Franciacorta will also be medium- to full-bodied, offering a creamy mouthfeel and a nose and palate that is more complex, while balancing fruit with minerality, yeastiness and nuttiness.

Franciacorta stands on its own as an aperitif or as an accompaniment to a rich meal, such as stuffed ravioli, pasta with white sauce or mushroom risotto. Don't even get us started on truffles, but when used in moderation in any rich or creamy dish, they make a beautiful accompaniment to a glass of Franciacorta.

Fizz Fact:

Franciacorta was the first DOC in Italy to require that its sparkling wines be made by the "Metodo Classico," or Traditional Method. The local consortium introduced stringent quality and production standards, resulting in the elevation of the DOC to a DOCG in 1995. Today, you won't find DOC Franciacorta wines.

ASTI

Grape Varieties
Moscato Bianco

Production Method
Charmat Method
(Single Fermentation)

Price Point
$

Primary Aromas & Flavours

- Peach
- Pear
- Honeysuckle
- Melon
- Apple Blossom

Sweetness

Dry   Sweet

Body

Light-Bodied   Full-Bodied

Acidity

Low   High

Alcohol

Low   High

Serving Temperature
4 - 7°C

Glassware
Flute or Tulip Glass

Cellaring Potential
None

Sparkling Spotlight: Asti

Asti is a sweet sparkling wine with an interesting story that may prove to be a cautionary tale for other sparkling-wine-producing regions. Once extremely popular due to its approachable price and fruity profile, Asti became a victim of its own success with a reputation of being sickly sweet and of poor quality. Sound familiar? Recently, an emphasis on quality and innovation in winemaking have made a difference for Asti in its bid to recapture a piece of the sparkling wine market.

Geography

Produced in northern Italy's Piedmont region, including the town of Asti (from which it gets its name), Asti is a more significant export for the region than either Barolo or Barbaresco. How large? Try 50 million bottles, of which 85% is exported.

While the viticultural areas of Piedmont have a long history, sparkling winemaking is a relatively recent innovation. Work by the local consortium began in the 1930s and interest in Asti increased after the Second World War. It grew significantly into the 1970s before taking a nosedive in popularity as consumers sought drier sparkling wines. Despite this trend, production volumes remain high to this day, with Asti DOCG introducing rigorous standards to improve the reputation of its wines.

Production

Asti is made from the Moscato Bianco grape, a white wine grape known for its small berries, tight clusters, and aromatic profile. Unlike many other sparkling wines, Asti does not undergo a secondary fermentation. Instead, a single fermentation takes place in a pressurized stainless-steel tank. The carbon dioxide produced during fermentation remains trapped in the tank. Shortly after, the tank is cooled down to stop fermentation early. The wine is filtered before bottling, and contains a lower amount of pressure than most other sparkling wines.

Fizz Fact:

Both Asti and Moscato d'Asti DOCG share Moscato Bianco as their principal grape. Wines made in the Moscato d'Asti DOCG are still (though they may have the slightest effervescence), and are known for their musky, floral and fruity aromas, low alcohol content and sweet profile.

Profile and Character

A question we often get asked: is Asti really that sweet?

As fermentation is stopped early, a considerable amount of sugar remains, resulting in a sweeter wine. An Asti wine will also generally be lower in alcohol and have intense floral and fruity aromas. This aromatic profile is a signature for this wine style.

While Asti may be enjoyed as an aperitif, or an accompaniment to light fare, we think it is ideally suited as a companion to, or replacement for, dessert.

LAMBRUSCO

Grape Varieties
Lambrusco

Production Method
Various (Charmat Method
is the most common)

Price Point
$

Primary Aromas & Flavours

- Strawberry
- Black Cherry
- Cola
- Rhubarb
- Rose

Sweetness

Dry   Sweet

Body

Light-Bodied   Full-Bodied

Acidity

Low   High

Alcohol

Low   High

Serving Temperature
7 - 10°C

Glassware
Red or White Wine Glass

Cellaring Potential
None

Sparkling Spotlight: Lambrusco

As the world's best sparkling wines are typically produced in cooler climates, it should come as no surprise that you'll find less being made as you travel further south in Italy. The most southerly portion of what would be considered northern Italy is known for red sparkling wine: *Lambrusco*. This wine style has recently seen a resurgence in both interest and popularity (after taking a hit in the late 1980s, when it was synonymous with bulk wine production).

Geography

Produced in the hilly, temperate Emilia-Romagna region, Lambrusco is a red sparkling wine made from the grape of the same name. Or, we should say, grapes, as Lambrusco is an umbrella term encapsulating various expressions of the same grape, several of which are covered by their own DOC. Most Lambrusco is made under the region-wide Lambrusco Emilia IGT. How much? About 125 million bottles of IGT compared to 41 million bottles of DOC.

Production

The wine can be produced in the Traditional, Charmat or Ancestral Method, with most made in the Charmat Method.

You may be familiar with the sweeter style popularized in the 1980s. However, Lambrusco wines may also be dry. Drier Lambrusco is becoming more common and producers using the Traditional and Ancestral Methods are yielding interesting results.

Profile & Character

A red sparkling wine will stand out not only in terms of its colour profile – which will be opaque and usually deep red or garnet – but also for its aroma and flavour. Lambrusco will typically be aromatic and full of ripe red fruits, vanilla cola and violets, though variations exist as a result of the production method used. Some will express fresher red fruits.

Overall, Lambrusco is meant to be enjoyed young, so cellaring is unnecessary. Lambrusco can be enjoyed as an aperitif, but its fuller-bodied profile makes it a great match with heartier fare. We're thinking pasta Bolognese, lasagna, a panino or our favourite food pairing, a simple pepperoni pizza.

TRENTODOC

Grape Varieties
Chardonnay, Pinot
Noir, Pinot Meunier
& Pinot Blanc

Production Method
Traditional

Price Point
$$

Primary Aromas & Flavours
- Citrus
- Yellow Apple
- Almond
- Honeysuckle
- Minerality

Sweetness

Dry   Sweet

Body

Light-Bodied   Full-Bodied

Acidity

Low   High

Alcohol

Low   High

Serving Temperature
7 - 10°C

Glassware
White Wine or Tulip Glass

Cellaring Potential
3 - 5 Years

Sparkling Spotlight: Trentodoc

Franciacorta's unofficial title as the "Champagne of Italy" now has a serious challenger in Trento. While we aren't fans of this comparison, we are big fans of the Traditional Method wines from this region.

The founders of what is now Trento DOC wanted to distinguish themselves from Prosecco, which is produced in relative proximity, and therefore you won't find any Charmat tanks or Glera grapes used in wines from this region.

Geography

Trento DOC, or *Trentodoc*, is a northern Italian appellation centred around the city of Trento (approximately halfway between Venice and Milan). Generally, the area has an alpine topography and a cooler climate, making it well suited to produce sparkling wine.

Production

Permitted grapes in Trentodoc include Chardonnay, Pinot Noir, Pinot Meunier and Pinot Blanc. Wines in this appellation may only be made in the Traditional Method.

Trentodoc also applies additional standards and regulations to harvest and to the finished wines made within the appellation. About 10,000 hectares (24,700 acres) of the region is under vine, with about 1,000 hectares (2,470 acres) yielding grapes for sparkling wines. The region produces about nine million bottles per year, significantly smaller than Prosecco, Asti, Lambrusco and even Franciacorta.

Minimum aging time sur lie also applies: 15 months for non-vintage, 24 months for vintage, and 36 months for riserva wines. For reference, Franciacorta – Italy's other major Traditional Method wine region – requires additional time sur lie for non-vintage and riserva wines.

Profile and Character

Like other wines made in the Traditional Method (from the same or similar grape varieties), the sparkling wines from Trentodoc will be dry with a delicate perlage. They are characterized by a rich and complex bouquet of citrus, tree fruit, yeastiness, and almond. Rosé sparkling wines from Trentodoc will generally showcase tart red fruit and berries on the nose and palate.

You may find examples of Trentodoc wines are exceptional value. Matching complexity with an approachable and easy to enjoy profile, Trentodoc wines can be enjoyed as an aperitif and will stand up to light and heartier fare. Whether a brunch, a seasonal barbecue or a rich, multi-layered holiday dinner, a glass of Trentodoc can hold its own, while elevating the everyday.

Sparkling Reflections: Italy

Italy is a beautiful country to visit.

Topping our list is the wine region around Valdobbiadene, just to the north of Venice, where Prosecco is produced. From the incredibly scenic, impossibly sloped vineyards, to the wineries and historic villages nestled among the foothills of the Alpine-Dolomite mountain ranges, it's a breathtaking place and it's no wonder that this area was declared a UNESCO World Heritage Site.

So, how could we top off an amazing Prosecco adventure? Well, with a rustic farmhouse full of bread, cheese, cured meats and Prosecco, of course!

Osteria Senz'Oste, known for its "pay what you can" approach to food and wine, is perhaps even more famous for another reason. After cautiously following wooden signs promising "Prosecco this way," we climbed past the Osteria and were face-to-face with one of man's greatest achievements: a Prosecco vending machine.

After popping in a €20 note and grabbing a bottle of wine, we bought some cheese and bread with the change. Then we enjoyed the simple and rustic food pairing, along with the summer sun and sweeping views of Valdobbiadene. We can't wait to go back! – Mike

Chapter 10:

SPAIN

Cava

Picturesque Penedès 06/2012

A Sparkling Winos dream car!

Spain: An Introduction

You maybe be familiar with the term "Cava" – Spain's famous bubbly. You may have even enjoyed a glass of it at some point in your life, perhaps on New Year's Eve, a birthday celebration or while in Spain, lapping up the sunshine and tapas.

Cava is a brand with global name recognition.

While you can find Cava almost anywhere, you won't find it on the map in the way you would Champagne (or Prosecco, for that matter). Cava has historically been less about place and more about style. It can be produced across Spain (though it's primarily concentrated in Catalonia).

But why is that, and what is Cava exactly?

Let's get into it and discover what makes this Spanish sparkling wine so special.

CAVA

Grape Varieties
Macabeo, Parellada
& Xarel·lo

Production Method
Traditional

Price Point
$

Primary Aromas & Flavours

- Citrus
- Almond
- Quince
- Toast
- Minerality

Sweetness

Dry   Sweet

Body

Light-Bodied   Full-Bodied

Acidity

Low   High

Alcohol

Low   High

Serving Temperature
6 - 8°C

Glassware
White Wine or Tulip Glass

Cellaring Potential
1 - 3 Years

Sparkling Spotlight: Cava

Ah, Cava. Spain's – or should we say, Catalonia's – venerable sparkling wine has been enjoyed the world over. And we mean it: Freixenet, the largest producer of Cava, claims its Cordon Negro is the world's most imported sparkling wine. This iconic black bottle has been a fixture at many celebrations, meals, and get-togethers we've attended over the years.

Cava's ubiquity, approachability and budget-friendly price have led some to call it Spain's answer to Prosecco. However, its history, method of production, and profile would lead us to (respectfully) disagree!

Geography

Cava was once referred to as "Spanish Champagne," but as wine appellation and labelling laws evolved, regulators and winemakers adopted the term "Cava" (meaning "cave" or "cellar" in Spanish) to differentiate themselves from Champagne. The first reference to Cava was in 1952, though regulations only followed a few decades later.

Most Cava is made in Catalonia, with 95% of total production being produced in the hilly, chalky, and coastal Penedès region (about 45 minutes inland from the beautiful coastal city of Barcelona in northeastern Spain). Its hills and coastal climate contribute to favourable conditions to produce sparkling wine.

Cava holds *Denominación de Origen (DO)* status in Spain, meaning it must be produced following specific guidelines (and within a defined geographic border) in order to bear the name Cava on the label. The Cava DO is quite large, taking in an area to the north and west of Barcelona (referred to as the Comtats de Barcelona). Central within this area is the charming town of Sant Sadurní d'Anoia, which, with its historic core and many urban sparkling wine houses and production facilities, is sometimes called the "Capital of Cava." Many major producers, such as Freixenet and Codorníu, who account for the lion's share of production and exports, are located here.

Despite its heart being in Sant Sadurní d'Anoia, Cava can – for historical reasons – be made in other parts of Spain. These areas include the Ebro Valley (northern Spain), Viñedos de Almendralejo (southern Spain, near the city of Badajoz) and the Levante Zone (near the city of Valencia). These areas, however, only account for approximately 5% of total output.

In 2020, within the Comtats de Barcelona and Ebro Valley Zones, the Cava DO has permitted the creation of sub-zones to recognize unique terroirs and microclimates, and support product differentiation. Only time will tell which of these sub-zones will sparkle brightest!

Sparkling Spotlight:

Anaïs Manobens Mora
Proprietor & Winemaker
Maria Rigol Ordi

We asked Anaïs, "What makes Cava so special?"

"I would say that for me Cava is past (tradition), present (life) and future (challenge). Cava is our most gastronomic wine, a great sparkling wine that stands out for the great quality it offers. This makes it a sparkling wine capable of competing with the best sparkling wines in the world. Our Mediterranean varieties and our way of doing things also imprints a unique character and identity that we have to explain and communicate, here and beyond our borders."

Sparkling Spotlight:

Olivia Junyent
Proprietor & Winemaker
Castell D'Age

We asked Olivia, "What makes Cava so special?"

"Its careful production method, its quality, the typicity of its varieties and its long-aging. Cava is elegant, versatile and unique."

Sparkling Spotlight:

Laia Esmel
Proprietor & Winemaker
Cava Esmel

We asked Laia, "What makes Cava so special?"

"The Traditional Method which is also made by other wine regions, reflects a territory mainly in the autonomous community of Catalonia. Cava is culture, tradition and sharing."

Production

Cava is a Traditional Method sparkling wine. Compared to other wine appellations where this method is predominant, aging times in the Cava DO are shorter. Cava must age a minimum of nine months, with Cava Reserva aging a minimum of 18 months and Cava Gran Reserva and Cava de Paraje Calificado aging at least 30 and 36 months, respectively.

It can be made using a blend of Macabeo, Parellada and Xarel·lo grapes, considered by many to be the three signature grapes of the Cava DO.

Let's meet this special trio.

Macabeo, also known as Viura, is a white wine grape grown across Spain and southern France and is known for its high productivity, fresh, fruity, mildly acidic profile, and aging potential. Some consider it the workhorse of the Cava trio. Parellada is also a white wine grape, and it brings much needed florality and white tree fruit aromas to the blend. Last, but not least, is Xarel·lo, a white wine grape renowned for its acidity. You may think that we're putting too much emphasis on acid, but when it comes to sparkling wine, acidity is critical!

This classic Cava blend is not alone in flying the flag. Compared to other appellations, the Cava DO is relatively permissive when it comes to grape varieties that can be used. Chardonnay and Pinot Noir are also permitted, along with Garnacha, Subirat Parent, Trepat and Monastrell (also known as Mourvèdre).

The red wine grapes permitted in the DO – Pinot Noir, Garnacha, Trepat and Monastrell – produce Cava Rosado, or Rosé Cava. It must be made in the Rosé Saignée method, during which the skins have contact with the must, adding colour. You will find that Rosé Cava expresses different shades of pink, from onion skin to raspberry.

Aside from being big geographically, Cava is big business. In 2020, almost 215 million bottles of Cava were produced. However, as significant as this production was, it represents a nearly 14% drop from 2019. Will production increase again? It will be interesting to watch, that's for sure.

Profile & Characteristics

Cava is a light- to medium-bodied, typically dry, sparkling wine with zesty citrus flavours, a distinct minerality and racy acidity. A Cava aged longer on the lees will often develop a beautiful baked apple note and a pronounced nuttiness.

As it is made in the Traditional Method, the perlage will be fine and it will have a lovely, lively *mousse* which contributes to a smooth and creamy mouth feel.

In terms of sweetness, Cava can range from Brut Nature (0-3 grams of sugar per litre) to Dulce (50+ grams of sugar per litre). Brut Cava (up to 12 grams of sugar per litre) is the most common style, though Brut Nature Cava is popular domestically.

For Brut Cava, dominant flavours typically include citrus, quince, almond, and tart apple. Secondary flavours often include brioche, fig, and, as a hallmark of the style, a chalky minerality. For Rosé Cava, dominant flavours will include red fruit and cherry and apple blossom.

Fizz Fact:

Riddling, the process of tilting and turning bottles in a rack to ensure the lees collect in the neck of the bottle (allowing disgorgement), is time-consuming when done by hand and adds significant cost to a Traditional Method sparkling wine. Several decades ago, Cava producers helped pioneer a technological advancement in sparkling wine production with the invention of the gyropalette.

If the name wasn't impressive enough, its ultimate purpose sure is!

Essentially, a gyropalette is a machine that automates the riddling of large cages containing wine bottles, making the process quick and efficient. From a consumer perspective, it has helped lower the cost of some sparkling wines, including Cava.

Fizz Fact:

The Raventós family name is virtually synonymous with Cava. In the 1870s, the family was instrumental in pivoting their winery to the production of Traditional Method sparkling wine, kickstarting local interest and, some say, the Cava DO. That winery - Codorníu - is now the oldest and second-largest producer of Cava.

As successful as Cava has become globally, some suggest there is a need to return to the traditions that made it so great in the first place.

With Raventós i Blanc, descendants of Codorníu's founders are trailblazing their way toward this goal through the Conca del Riu Anoia DO, reflecting a small geographical area centred around the River Anoia Basin. In this DO, winegrowing requirements are stricter with only native grape varieties (no Pinot Noir and Chardonnay are permitted) and increased minimum aging times. Many producers have criticized the creation of a new DO, but its members are growing each year. Only time will tell, however, if Conca will conquer Cava.

Sparkling Reflections: Spain

Barcelona is one of the most picturesque cities in the world: from its beautiful beaches to its unbelievable architecture, to the wonderful people and food, there is something here for everyone.

As we learned on a trip several years ago, Cava is enjoyed throughout the day and on any – or no – occasion in Catalonia's capital. We stumbled upon a small bar called El Xampanyet somewhere near Barcelona's Gothic Quarter where tapas dishes were accompanied by coupes of Cava – poured not only from bottles but also casks. We stayed for a glass (or several) and were inspired to visit a few producers in the region.

We quickly found some Wi-Fi, did some research, and booked train tickets to Sant Sadurní d'Anoia for the next day.

Emerging from the train station and (pretty much) walking straight into Freixenet, we found our experience to be personal (given the magnitude of the operation), and the level of detail about the history of Cava, its production and the wines was impressive. I don't think I'll ever get over the scale of production and the number of active *gyropalettes*.

As for Codorníu, after a fair jaunt in the summer heat through red, mineral-rich soils, we made it to what felt like an oasis.

It's fair to say that the Modernista-style architectural gem designed by prolific Catalan architect Josep Puig i Cadafalch was the most beautiful winery I've ever visited. It felt appropriate to appreciate its majestic splendour with a glass of Cava. You certainly couldn't do that inside Antoni Gaudí's Sagrada Família! – Mike

Chapter 11:

GERMANY

Hand disgorging in Pfalz 02/2019

Sparkling in Düsseldorf

Sparkling Spotlight: Germany

When you think of German wine, what comes to mind?

Is it the iconic slopes of the Mosel valley, with its historic towns and centuries-long tradition of viticulture? Is it Riesling – king of the German wine scene? Or maybe Spätburgunder (Pinot Noir) from Southwest Germany? Eiswein, perhaps?

We're here to tell you that *Sekt*, Germany's criminally underappreciated sparkling wine, should be on your radar. And in your glass.

Sekt

In Germany, sparkling wine is known as Sekt. Although Germans are known for their love of sparkling wine, including their native product, Sekt is not well represented outside its local market (except, perhaps, for the omnipresent Henkell Trocken and Rotkäppchen-Mumm). But just how much do the Germans love Sekt?

Annual per capita consumption of sparkling wine in Deutschland is the highest in the world. When it comes to expenditure on alcoholic beverages per household, Germans spent on average more than 7% on sparkling wine from 2016 through 2019. Despite wine consumption dropping during this period, Sekt consumption remained stable.

Geography

German interest in Sekt is long-standing.

Some would say German sparkling wine stands in the shadow of Champagne, but the Germans have had an imprint on many Champagne houses: Bollinger, Krug, and Mumm, to name a few. This connection helped bring Champagne's expertise to Germany, where winemakers desired to make sparkling wine more efficiently – this is Germany we're talking about, after all. Moving up the historical narrative to the end of the First World War in 1918, several treaties were signed which restricted the use of the term "Champagne," and from then, the term "Sekt" took off.

Sekt can be produced in any of Germany's 13 wine regions. Except for Saale-Unstrut and Sachsen in the eastern part of the country, the remainder are located primarily in the south and southwest, where moderate summer temperatures predominate and provide excellent conditions for viticulture. The south and southwest produce a significant proportion of Sekt.

Sparkling Spotlight:

Alexia Putze and Mark Barth
Proprietors & Winemakers
Wein und Sektgut Barth

We asked Alexia and Mark, "What makes Sekt so special?"

"Wine is a great product – and accompanying the journey from the vineyard to the glass is certainly one of the most diverse professions I know. To produce a sparkling wine from a still wine is for me the supreme discipline. For over 30 years we have been producing sparkling wine according to the Traditional Method in our own cellar. We aim for elegant and balanced sparkling wines that radiate an inner peace through slow and natural aging as well as extra-long yeast storage. Our single-vineyard sparkling wines should reflect the Rheingau origin in all facets. Predestined for this style is our home grape variety – the Riesling!"

Production

So, what's the story behind Sekt being such a big deal in Germany? There's a bit of a geheimnis, or secret, here.

Sekt is not a protected term in the way that Champagne, Cava or Prosecco are. It can be made in various ways, including the Traditional Method, the Charmat Method and, in some cases, force carbonation. Many of the large, internationally known brands (like the aforementioned Henkell Trocken and Rotkäppchen-Mumm) will utilize cost-effective methods to make Sekt. They are permitted to import base wines from outside Germany (with Italian and Spanish bulk wine supporting Sekt production indirectly).

The varieties used in Sekt production include Riesling, Silvaner, Weissburgunder (Pinot Blanc), Grauburgunder (Pinot Gris), Schwarzriesling (Pinot Meunier), Spätburgunder (Pinot Noir) and Chardonnay. You may also find other German grape varieties used. We should also note that Sekt will typically be made from a single grape variety, rather than a blend, and approximately half of premium Sekt is made from – you guessed it – Riesling.

As a Sekt-head, it can be tough to decipher which wines are produced using grapes grown in Germany, which will give you the most genuine expression of local production and terroir.

When looking at a bottle of Sekt, the label should help us decipher what we are about to enjoy: Deutscher Sekt denotes a sparkling wine made from 100% German grapes. Sekt b.A. or Qualitätsschaumwein b.A indicates wine from an appellation of origin and is labelled accordingly (b.A. indicating from a specified region). When at least 85% of the wine originates from an appellation, a smaller geographical unit is also permitted on the label, such as a vineyard. If at least 85% of the wine is of a specific vintage or grape variety, a vintage or grape variety may be named on the label. And finally, if you see Winzersekt on the label, this means you have in your hands a vintners' vintage, varietal, sparkling wine that was produced by a winemaker or co-operative using grapes grown themselves. These must be made in the Traditional Method only. In this case, the vintage, grape variety, and producer's name must appear on the bottle.

In the case of Winzersekt, approximately 10% of all German sparkling production is vintage or varietal sparkling wine. These are produced across Germany's many wine regions, offering exciting insight into terroir and winemaking approaches. Of the German Winzersekt, it is perhaps unsurprising that most are Riesling. With racy, pronounced acidity, Riesling Winzersekt is undoubtedly something special. And we have to say, they are Köstlich (that is, delicious)!

Touching on sugar, a topic that often comes up when discussing German wines (and Riesling in particular), we'd like to emphasize this: not all Sekt is sweet. In fact, labelling is like other regions, with Sekt being made across the sweetness spectrum from Naturherb (Brut Nature, 0-3 grams per litre) to Mild (Doux, 50 grams per litre and over).

Profile & Characteristics

Though there's a lot to say about Sekt, given the diversity, we will focus on Winzersekt – high-quality sparkling wine from a single vintage, a single grape variety or Pinot-based cuvée, and made in the Traditional Method with a minimum of nine months on the lees.

As we have enjoyed seeing in Germany, Winzersekt producers are passionate about their product. While Sekt may not be a protected term, Winzersekt producers are crafting high-quality Riesling and Pinot-based sparkling wine that speak to a particular sense of place and bring an inherent "Germanness" to the wine. We can't think of a more German wine than Riesling-based Winzersekt!

Most Winzersekt producers are small, and they craft their wine with care and by hand (including disgorgement, which we had the chance to have, uh, a hand in). It certainly was a different world visiting producers such as Bamberger, Sekt & Weingut Winterling, Sekthaus Krack and Weingut Weinreich, whose production remains at a human scale, compared to Rotkäppchen-Mumm, which utilizes a 33-metre-long machine that labels and caps 30,000 bottles an hour.

But we digress.

From the elegant, finessed, and long-lasting Rieslings to the rich and powerful Pinot blends, Winzersekt is something seriously special and inherently German. It rivals the best sparkling wine in the world.

Fizz Fact:

Germany has 13 wine regions where Sekt may be made as the term is not protected. We'd be remiss not to mention a few of these wine regions:

Rheinhessen is Germany's largest wine region. Lying in a valley of gently rolling hills, the region comprises steep vineyard sites with varied soils and favourable climatic conditions, making it possible to grow a wide range of grape varieties. Wines are often described as soft, fragrant, and easy drinking, however there are plenty of premium examples that exude elegance, depth and complexity.

The Pfalz is Germany's second-largest wine region but typically has the largest crop of all. Riesling is king here, producing wines with great substance and finesse. Modern technology and viticultural practices have considerably impacted the region in the past 40 or so years.

Despite being one of Germany's smallest wine regions, Nahe has an impressive range of diverse soil types, resulting in some seriously complex and exciting wines. The steeper sites are rich in volcanic soil, producing elegant and mineral-driven Rieslings (the most widespread grape variety in the region). Most of the wineries in Nahe have a relatively small production, and many of them were family farms before they became wineries.

Sparkling Reflections: Germany

In January 2019, I had the pleasure of visiting Germany on a Sekt-tacular trip through several regions, including Nahe, Pfalz and Rheingau.

Focussed on Sekt, the trip was a sparkling whirlwind: in four days, I visited four different German wine regions, tasted over 100 German sparkling wines, and, on top of that, helped to select the best Sekt in all of Germany. Not an average January, even for a Sparkling Wino!

My journey began with a trip to the Wines of Germany headquarters in Bodenheim. My first task was judging and then selecting the Top 20 Sekt in all of Germany. No big deal, right?

The German Wine Institute put out an open call for premium examples of German sparkling wine, and they received 250+ submissions. As a member of an expert panel, I tasted and scored the Institute's pre-selected 44 samples blind. The Top 20 selected were then poured at ProWein 2019 in Düsseldorf. It was an honour to be a part of this tasting panel and then taste the top contender again in the spring at one of the world's largest wine expositions. Still pinching myself … if only I could remember what the top pick was! – Jeff

Chapter 12:

ENGLAND

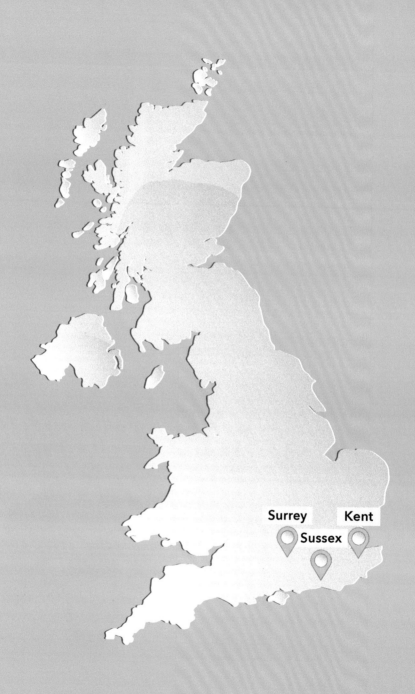

Press at ProWein 03/2019

English fizz galore!

Sparkling Spotlight: England

Some say that the English were responsible for Champagne becoming a global brand. We're not sure we believe that in its entirety, but English ingenuity and trade did expand Champagne producers' reach during the industrial revolution. The fondness for fizz in Britain is undeniable and persists to this day. Full of interested consumers with buying power, the isle is now also home to many producers who specialize in the production of sparkling wine. But can the United Kingdom become a new sparkling kingdom?

English Sparkling Wine

Only time will tell if English sparkling will fizz, or fizzle in the global marketplace. In the meantime, there's no reason not to taste some English bubbly and decide for yourself if this is a category worth exploring.

Geography

It's fair to say that while private viticulture has had a long history in England, the modern wine industry is nascent, but with significant growth in the past 50 years.

The south of England has geological features, chalky soils, and climate resembling France's Champagne region. This makes it ideal for Traditional Method sparkling wine production. Most producers are in England's southeast (concentrated in Kent, West and East Sussex, and Surrey). Marquee producers such as Nyetimber, Gusbourne Estate and Chapel Down anchor this area. The Southwest is England's second largest area for sparkling wine production.

Production

In Great Britain, the pragmatic "English Sparkling Wine" applies to wines made in the Traditional Method. However, from some of the English Sparkling Wines we've enjoyed, we've gleaned that a number of producers prefer more compelling branding, using terms such as "Britagne" and "Méthode Britannique" on their bottles. More recently, the national wine marketing association introduced the phrase "Classic Method Sparkling Wine," supported by a "Great British Classic Method" hallmark and campaign, to further differentiate Traditional Method sparkling wine produced in England and Wales. As of 2021, further regulations associated with the term were planned, and it remains to be seen if the hallmark resonates with consumers in the United Kingdom and across the world.

English and Welsh wine is protected by Protected Designation of Origin (PDO) status as determined by the European Union (and the United Kingdom, post-Brexit). Likewise, a more specific English and Welsh Regional Wine Protected Geographical Indication (PGI) is also in place.

The PDO's specifications for grapes for English Sparkling Wine are more restrictive than the PGI, permitting only the use of Chardonnay, Pinot Noir, Pinot Meunier, Pinot Blanc and Pinot Gris. Interestingly, in both the PDO and the PGI, de-acidification of cuvées intended for English Sparkling Wine is permitted without limit. It's fair to say that sparkling wine lovers should embrace the acidity, but some tempering of that electric acidity is required when it comes to English wines!

Overall, England and Wales are home to 700 vineyards and over 160 wineries, which in 2017 produced almost 6 million bottles of wine. Approximately 70% of that production is sparkling wine.

English Sparkling Wine remains niche despite the industry's growth: only one in five British consumers reported tasting it in 2020. This is while the United Kingdom ranks as one of the largest markets for sparkling wine globally (with approximately 200 million bottles of sparkling wines consumed over the same period).

Profile & Characteristics

When made in the Traditional Method, English Sparkling Wine will likely be made from one or a blend of three core varieties: Chardonnay, Pinot Noir and Pinot Meunier. Coupled with the similarity in climate and soils between the south of England (where most producers are located) and the Champagne region, this will result in a similar profile between the wines of the two regions.

However, while Champagne can be emulated, we are firm believers that it cannot be replicated. English Sparkling Wines tends to have higher acidity (given the cooler climate) and, based on our experience, will have less of an autolytic character (complexity and creaminess imparted by lees contact). Nonetheless, the category is exciting and worth exploring.

Sparkling Spotlight:

Emma Rice
Head Winemaker

Hattingley Valley Wines

We asked Emma, "What makes English Sparkling Wine so special?"

"We are at the frontier of viable grape-growing and winemaking here in the UK. With a cool climate we are perfectly positioned to produce high quality Traditional Method sparkling wines that have huge aging potential. The real markers for English Sparkling Wine are an intense purity of fruit character supported by elegant, linear acidity, both of which come from the long, cool growing season. Hattingley Valley employs a judicious use of older oak barrels to soften and round out the wines, giving them a generosity that appeals to a wide audience."

Sparkling Reflections: England

Though we have not had the pleasure of visiting England to taste English Sparkling Wine, we have had the pleasure of tasting some exceptional examples from the comfort of our own home and at ProWein in 2019.

Back in 2019, English fizz was on the rise, with a whole lot of excellent press and plenty of praise among our sparkling wine crew. We had tasted a few notable examples available in our market, but we were so excited to sample some other well-known but, as yet, unrepresented producers. So, despite the doom and gloom around the then-looming Brexit, we approached the English Wine booth at ProWein with sheer delight.

We were introduced to sparkling producers hailing from all over the United Kingdom, including South Downs, Ashford and Pulborough. If your familiarity with the geography of England is limited to London, let's just say south of there and north of the English Channel, ok?

Standouts for us were East Sussex's Ridgeview, which has been pioneering English sparkling for over twenty years. Hot on the heels of winning Winemaker of the Year at the International Wine & Spirit Competition 2018 (and making history for English wine, no less), Ridgeview's dream of producing world-class sparkling wine appeared to have come to fruition. We particularly liked the Ridgeview Bloomsbury, a blend of Chardonnay, Pinot Noir and Meunier. Electric, with notes of tree fruit and honey, we weren't surprised to learn that this was the official wine served for the Queen's Diamond Jubilee! – Mike

Fizz Fact:

Christopher Merret (or Merrett), a 17th-century English physician and scientist, had many accomplishments, including studying both glassmaking and sparkling winemaking. He was one of the first to identify that adding sugar to wine helped increase its effervescence. Through his primary interest in glassmaking, he inspired industrialists to produce bottles strong enough to contain wines going through their often-volatile secondary fermentation. To that, we say cheers!

Chapter 13:

CANADA

British Columbia

Nova Scotia

Ontario

VOA Promoters-at-Large 06/2019

Wandering through wine country

Sparkling Spotlight: Canada

Canadian … wine? That's right!

There is more to Canada than maple syrup, hockey, scenic landscapes, and winter. For us, wine is at the forefront of the conversation, and there is so much to discover beyond the quintessentially Canadian export of Icewine. Though this luscious dessert wine has put Canada's wine industry on the map, so let's not understate its importance.

Like most of the Canadian population, the country's principal wine regions (located in the provinces of Ontario, British Columbia and Nova Scotia) are situated close to the country's southern border, shared with the United States. While generally in the south, Canada's wine regions are spread out across the country's 9.9 million square kilometres. In fact, there are around 4,500 kilometres (or 2,800 miles) between them – so each region is vastly different. On a global scale, Canada's wine-growing regions are small – comprising just under 12,000 hectares (or just under 30,000 acres), supporting about 500 wineries.

There are several unique viticultural areas within each region, all generally located on the same ideal grape growing latitudes as much of central France. From coast to coast, Canadians crafting sparkling wine are putting the cool in cool-climate viticulture.

So, let's get exploring, eh!

ONTARIO

Sparkling Spotlight: Ontario

We may be biased as Ontario is home, but wine country here is unlike anywhere else we've had the pleasure of visiting.

Really, we mean it!

There's so much to love about Ontario's wine country, starting with the rich array of winery properties themselves. Then there are the beautiful rural, natural landscapes and, finally, the towns rich in historic charm.

Global expressions may have sparked our love of sparkling wine, but our fondness for all things local remains firm. Some incredible bubbles are being made just a stone's throw from Toronto (and much of southern Ontario, for that matter).

Geography

While still a small viticultural region (coming in at about 6,900 hectares or 17,000 acres), Ontario is the largest wine region in Canada. Though its history dates back to plantings of labrusca and hybrid grapes in the 1800s, the region's modern era is often noted as starting in 1974 when the first winery license since the 1920s (coinciding with the era of Prohibition) was granted. Many winemaking pioneers followed, with *Vitis vinifera* plantings cropping up across the landscape.

Ontario subscribes to an appellation system and regulations defined by the *Vintners Quality Alliance (VQA)*, which speaks to the origin, quality, and authenticity of local wine. A bottle of VQA Ontario wine is made from 100% Ontario-grown grapes, differentiating itself from an International-Canadian Blend wine, which is blended and cellared in Canada primarily from imported grapes or juice.

The province is divided into three appellations: Niagara Peninsula, Prince Edward County and Lake Erie North Shore. All three are defined by geographic position – roughly between 41- and 44-degrees north latitude, a trait shared with Champagne and Burgundy. Winters are – wait for it – cold, but summers are hot, and the moderating effect of the Great Lakes has a beneficial impact on grape growing.

The Niagara Peninsula is divided into two regional appellations and further broken down into 10 sub-appellations, each with its unique character. Here, the Niagara Escarpment, the Niagara River and Lake Ontario are the defining influences. The area is home to a rich array of soil types, perfect for growing many Vitis vinifera varieties. Considered by some to be the heartland of Ontario's wine industry, the Niagara Peninsula is bookended by the beautiful town of Niagara-on-the-Lake in the east and the thriving, industrial city of Hamilton in the west. And no, we won't get into the rivalry between the Niagara Escarpment and Niagara-on-the-Lake regional appellations, which are split by lovely St. Catharines. Let's keep it saintly, shall we?

The Prince Edward County appellation is the newest on the block, founded in 2007. Located east of Toronto on a peninsula, "the County" or "PEC," as it's affectionally called, is home to a significant amount of shoreline – approximately 800 kilometres (500 miles) of it, including beautiful parks and beaches. But it's not just the scenic beauty that makes this area special – it's the sweet spot of moderated temperatures, limestone-rich soils and winemaking industriousness, all of which lead to some very distinct wines.

The Lake Erie North Shore appellation benefits from the moderating effects of – you guessed it – Lake Erie. This southerly appellation also has a longer growing season, allowing ripening conditions that support more full-bodied red wines. You'll find the South Islands sub-appellation here, including Pelee Island (home to Ontario's first winery).

Winemakers here have helped to firmly establish the region's roots in the wine world by planting the appropriate Vitis vinifera for Ontario's climate and working with stringent regulatory standards.

Fizz Fact:

In 1991, Inniskillin's 1989 Icewine won Grand Prix d'Honneur at Bordeaux's famed Vinexpo. Some considered the event a gamechanger in the world's appetite and love of Icewine, which remains a big business in Ontario.

In fact, the province produces 90% of Canada's total output, mainly from Vidal, Riesling and Cabernet Franc. The delicious confection – made from grapes naturally frozen on the vine, resulting in a concentration of sugar, acid, and flavour - continues to shine as about 50% of all wine exports from Ontario are Icewine.

And, before you ask - yes, you can find examples of sparkling Icewine. Many wineries even produce sparkling wine with an Icewine dosage!

Sparkling Spotlight:

Craig McDonald
Vice-President – Winemaking

Andrew Peller Limited

We asked Craig, "What makes Ontario sparkling wine so special?"

"For me it's our extreme cool-climate, unique soils and the constant challenge in our vineyards that define sparkling wines in Ontario. Because we are pushed to the limits with no margin for error, our wines have a nervous tension and freshness rarely seen in other regions.

"Then layer in extended aging in bottle on lees, non-vintage blending and a clear focus on the drier style of sparkling, and you start to see the very fine and complex quality potential of Ontario emerge. It's also exciting to be a part of such a unified and collaborative industry – such as the Fizz Club for sparkling winemakers, organized at Brock University's Cool Climate Oenology and Viticulture Institute – with a clear technical and creative focus towards advancing the quality and appeal of our sparkling wines.

"As the custodian of very old base wines at Trius, I've been fortunate to experience the rewards of patience first-hand and know that with further aging of our wines the best is yet to come. Exciting times!"

Sparkling Spotlight:

Amélie Boury
*Vice-President – Winemaking,
Vineyard & Operations*
Château des Charmes

We asked Amélie, "What makes Ontario sparkling wine so special?"

"Ontario is one of the greatest and most challenging cool climate regions: a perpetual reinvention playground for winemakers. Chardonnay and Pinot Noir make an excellent base for our Traditional Method sparkling wines and suit the Niagara terroir. Cool nights result in keeping high acidity and therefore freshness in the base juice. The Traditional Method creates energy in the glass with a persistent bubble leading to a nose of green apple, lemon and brioche."

Sparkling Spotlight:

Jonas Newman
Proprietor, Grower & Winemaker
Hinterland Wine Co.

We asked Jonas, "What makes Ontario sparkling wine so special?"

"One of the great truths about wine is that it starts in the vineyard. In Prince Edward County, we are blessed with a harmony between the soils, climate and grape varietals that suit sparkling wine perfectly. Every year, we push ourselves to do more in the vineyard and less in the winery to produce wines that reflect this very special place that we are lucky to work in."

Production

Ontario's 6,900 hectares of vines produce about 22 million litres of wine (only a small portion is sparkling wine). As of March 2020, there were 180 wineries, a significant increase from 66 in 2003. While the number of sparkling wines produced is dynamic, we think it's great to see so many producers seizing the optimal conditions for sparkling winemaking and crafting such great local bubbles.

In terms of production method, there is a relatively even split between Traditional Method and Charmat Method wines in Ontario, although recently there has been a surge in Charmat Method sparkling wine production, along with interest in Ancestral Method wines as well.

Readily available examples of classic, Traditional Method sparkling wines from Ontario include Trius Brut, Henry of Pelham Cuvée Catharine and Château des Charmes Brut.

Fizz Fact:

The production of sparkling wine in Ontario dates to the onset of the local wine industry's modern era: the 1970s.

Back then, though, all sparkling wine talk was Champagne talk. In 1973, Ontario's liquor control board granted a Beamsville-based producer a licence to produce "authentic French-style Champagne made in Canada." In 1974, the Podamer Champagne Company made the first Chardonnay-based Traditional Method sparkling wine in the region (though it released a series of hybrid-grape-based sparkling wines as well).

Not too long after Niagara Escarpment-based Podamer, Newark Winery followed and planned for a large production of sparkling wine in Niagara-on-the-Lake. Newark Winery would eventually become Hillebrand and then Trius. Today, the winery is home to Canada's most extensive sparkling wine cellar, a selection of exceptional Traditional Method sparkling wines and a social-media-friendly sparkling wine tour.

But they aren't alone.

Prince Edward County's Hinterland Wine Co. is Ontario's first sparkling wine-focused winery. They are in good company: we mapped out Ontario's sparkling wines, and over 120 producers now make VQA bubbly. Now, that's something to celebrate!

Profile & Characteristics

Ontario's VQA regulations permit almost all the common Vitis vinifera varieties. Select hybrid grapes are also permitted, including Vidal.

Why is this important for Ontario sparkling wine?

In Ontario, you will find many Vitis vinifera grapes used to make sparkling wine, though the most common are Chardonnay, Pinot Noir, Riesling and the hybrid Vidal. Naturally, the grapes and the production method will each impact the profile of Ontario sparkling wine. VQA does not require a specific process, so sparkling wines can be made in the Traditional, Charmat or Ancestral Method. Each will produce vastly different bubbly (or, as we always say, plenty of exciting reasons to taste local)!

Fizz Fact:

Most sparkling wine in Ontario is produced in the Niagara Peninsula (home to that famous waterfall you may have heard about) and Prince Edward County, also a peninsula surrounded by Lake Ontario. This appellation sits on limestone bedrock and has stony soils. Vines here offer low yields and excellent fruit concentration. Being Ontario's most northerly appellation, the base of the vines must be buried in the winter to avoid frost damage. That takes some dedication, eh?

NOVA SCOTIA

Sparkling Spotlight: Nova Scotia

Ah, Nova Scotia. As one of Canada's scenic maritime provinces, this part of the country conjures up images of friendliness, oceanside lighthouses, cool sea breezes, high tides, saltwater taffy and delicious, buttery lobster rolls. Oh, and sparkling wine.

You might be thinking: there's Nova Scotian bubbly?!

Yes, and there's so much of it to explore and taste (side of clam chowder optional, of course).

Geography

It's not a fluke or fad that Nova Scotians have embraced wine. Grape production was noted back in the 1600s at the French settlement of Port-Royal (now called Annapolis Royal). Modern production took root in the 1970s with a handful of pioneers, many of whom are still making wine today. Sparkling wine production owes a high five to these pioneers and to L'Acadie Vineyards and Benjamin Bridge, who saw the potential for bubbles in this corner of Canada.

Like Canada's other cool-climate wine-producing areas, Nova Scotia's primary wine regions straddle the northern limit of the habitable zone for grapes. There are four wine-producing areas here – the Annapolis Valley, the Gaspereau Valley, the South Shore, and the Malagash Peninsula. Fortuitously, the Minas Basin of the Bay of Fundy offers moderating climate effects for Nova Scotian wine producers, and geological history has left behind mineral-rich soil.

Like most cool-climate regions, the backbone of the wine industry in Nova Scotia is formed by aromatic white wines. From the locally regarded Tidal Bay wines, made from a blend of Vitis vinifera and hybrid varieties, to still Rieslings and Chardonnays, to internationally regarded Traditional Method sparkling wines, Nova Scotia is punching above its weight (and size)!

Production

By all measures, Nova Scotia is the smallest of Canada's three major viticultural regions (or, perhaps, we should say the quaintest).

Comprised of approximately 400 hectares (or 1,000 acres) under vine across seven main wine-producing areas and supported by just under 20 wineries, the region is small but growing. Together, these wineries produce over 200,000 cases annually or just under two million litres.

Producing sparkling wines, as well as table wines and dessert wines, the region is known for its plantings of hybrids (including L'Acadie, Seyval Blanc and Marechal Foch). Planting and use of Vitis vinifera varieties are trending up, including Riesling, Chardonnay and Pinot Noir (which, coincidentally, are star players in bubbles).

Unlike Ontario and British Columbia, Nova Scotia does not subscribe to a regulating body.

Fizz Fact:

We think it's fair to say that a global pandemic has dulled some of the world's sparkle. However, Nova Scotians have found something to celebrate in 2021, as the province's first vineyard turned 410 years old!

Planted in 1611 in Port-Royal on a hillside inland, the vineyard hosted not only Vitis vinifera plantings but also the Order of Good Cheer – North America's first dinner club.

Sparkling Spotlight:

Jean-Benoit Deslauriers
Head Winemaker

Benjamin Bridge

We asked Jean-Benoit, "What makes Nova Scotia sparkling wine so special?"

"There is a storied correlation between cool climates and the emergence of great sparkling wines, and this connection is due, in part, to the prerequisite for modest sugar levels in grapes destined for an 'effervescent' future. More sugars at harvest would simply translate into a higher alcohol content, which in turn could deny the ethereal drinkability desirable in sparkling wines. In that regard, a most suitable microclimate for sparkling allows the ripening process to be extended and be all but accelerated. It is from that perspective that Nova Scotia's Bay of Fundy provides a climatic opportunity equally as improbable as its record-breaking status within the natural world.

"As the world's highest and most powerful tides displace a volume of water greater than the combined flow of all of earth's freshwater rivers combined, the most unique surrounding ecosystem is created as a result, and that special growing environment turns out to be a habitat of choice for sparkling grapes. The moderating effect resulting from the strong tidal activity naturally preserves the brightness and vibrancy desired to create the uplifting and energizing qualities fundamental to the sparkling wine experience. Perhaps most importantly, these unlikely and dramatic natural circumstances are directly behind Nova Scotia's lengthy extension of the growing season, leading to an elusive combination of freshness and textural richness, or the merger of opulence and weightlessness.

"Look for a sense of electric energy as the unmistakable signature of Nova Scotia's sparkling wines; they are directly connected to an unexpected ecosystem on the edge of the planet's most suspenseful tidal turmoil."

Profile & Characteristics

Though many factors influence the profile of sparkling wine made in Nova Scotia, we think aromatics and acidity are key defining characteristics.

Traditional Method sparkling wines made in Nova Scotia, whether from Vitis vinifera or hybrid varieties, will have an incredibly aromatic bouquet and electric acidity. Often, the distinct minerality of the Bay of Fundy-influenced soils will also be pronounced, as will the imprint of salinity.

Charmat and other sparkling styles will produce more fruit-driven wines, which will also tend to have a sweeter profile.

Fizz Fact:

You may see the name "L'Acadie" when experiencing Nova Scotian sparkling wines.

L'Acadie, or more formally L'Acadie Blanc, is a complex hybrid of several Vitis genus grapes and is sometimes referred to as Nova Scotia's answer to Chardonnay.

Created in Ontario - where it proved too warm for the grape to prosper - it was taken to Nova Scotia, where the terroir and climate proved to be a perfect match.

L'Acadie is found in vineyards across the province, including one of the local pioneers: L'Acadie Vineyards. They use the grape to craft exceptional Traditional Method sparkling wines.

We agree with the saying, "what grows together, goes together." We can't think of a more delicious pairing than a glass of L'Acadie's Traditional Method sparkling wine and a warm lobster roll.

BRITISH COLUMBIA

Sparkling Spotlight: British Columbia

Sweeping, unspoiled landscapes. Evergreens as far as the eye can see. Canada's only desert. These are just a few of British Columbia's assets.

Its wine regions – clustered around Lake Okanagan and along the Pacific Coast – are by all accounts some of the most beautifully located, warmest and productive.

But does sparkling wine shine here like in the rest of the country? You bet!

Geography

The wine regions of British Columbia are located at the northern extreme for optimal grape production. However, given the wine regions' latitude, climatic conditions are somewhat unexpected. They benefit from a unique climate with a short, hot growing season and desert-like conditions. Bet you didn't expect that in Canada!

The Okanagan Valley is the most well-known of the nine appellations in Canada's westernmost province. It's home to more than half of British Columbia's 280 or so wineries. The other appellations – located primarily along the province's southern border – include the Kootenays, Shuswap, Thompson Valley, Fraser Valley, Lillooet, Similkameen Valley, the Gulf Islands and Vancouver Island. As in Ontario, British Columbia subscribes to the VQA system, which prescribes the wine appellations and regulations.

Overall production is smaller than Ontario, with the area under vine in British Columbia coming in at just over 4,200 hectares (approximately 10,300 acres). The lion's share of that is within the Okanagan Valley – home to more than 170 wineries.

The Okanagan Valley wine region shares the same latitude as the Champagne region of France and the Rheingau in Germany. However, the continental climate, high daily temperatures and long hours of daylight make the Okanagan capable of producing diverse wines, from cool-climate whites to warmer-climate reds. The diversity of geographic conditions, higher altitudes, and generally warmer weather make the Okanagan Valley and most of British Columbia's other appellations distinct from Canada's other major viticultural areas.

There's a bit of sparkling history to tell, too. British Columbia's first sparkling wines were crafted on the mainland by the hands of the pioneering winemakers behind Steller's Jay. They were the first to produce a Traditional Method sparkling wine back in the late 1980s, followed later by Blue Mountain Winery.

Sparkling Spotlight:

David Paterson
Winemaker
Tantalus Vineyards

We asked David, "What makes British Columbia sparkling wine so special?"

"Sparkling wine in the Okanagan is experiencing a real renaissance right now, with more and more producers taking it seriously and giving it the deserving attention and patience. The Central and North regions of the Okanagan Valley always deliver wonderful nervy acidity and depth of texture which shows in the wines after élevage.

"At Tantalus, we have always been on a 'vintage style' program with our base wines typically aging in seasoned oak for 6-8 months before a 22-month tirage. Minimal dosage is needed to bring out the character and balance of the wines. Our vineyard site has long produced fine bubbly - hearkening back to the Pioneer Vineyard days with the Dulik family. We are immensely proud to carry on this tradition and we are seeing the real potential of sparkling wine off the property come to life, as they mature gracefully and become ever more compelling with time."

Production

British Columbia is home to a wide variety of sites, grapes and wines.

The most planted whites are Pinot Gris and Chardonnay, and the most planted reds are Merlot and Pinot Noir. Surprisingly, given the hype around British Columbia reds, the ratio of white to red plantings is so close – 49% to 51%.

British Columbia's fair climate means that it can support just about any grape variety, and with that freedom comes the challenge of focus. If they can grow everything, then what shines as a signature grape variety?

While the discussion around the signature grape variety for British Columbia is ongoing, we were impressed by the consideration given to sparkling wines in the Okanagan Valley.

Over 50 British Columbia producers make sparkling wines, which is an impressive feat!

The love of local is also impressive. In British Columbia, VQA wines continue to be the second best-selling category in the market, taking in an almost 20% share of overall sales. So, what's the best-selling category? It's not France, Italy or California. It's British Columbia's non-VQA wines (that is, International-Canadian Blends).

Fizz Fact:

British Columbia's wine regions have a higher proportion of growing degree days (GDD) – measured in degrees Celsius and defined as a measure of climate suitability, over a day, a month or a season – than many of the world's most famous wine regions.

At the top of the list is Osoyoos, located at the southern end of the Okanagan Valley, which accumulates just over 1,550 GDD during the growing season. Canadian counterpart Niagara, and world-renowned Napa, both collect approximately 1,450 GDD. Épernay, located in Champagne, accumulates 1,050 GDD.

Profile & Characteristics

So, what makes British Columbia bubbly special?

Unlike Ontario and Nova Scotia, which are both relatively flat, British Columbia is mountainous and with that comes diverse growing conditions. From steep slopes to sheltered valleys near lakes and rivers, British Columbia's wine regions also benefit from hot summer days and cool evenings in the fall.

The warmer climate in British Columbia leads to sparkling wines that are more fruit-driven, often with hints of marzipan and almond.

Fizz Fact:

Divine symmetry, apparently, is a thing. It ascribes symbolic and sacred meanings to specific geometric shapes and structures, such as pyramids. Are there pyramids in British Columbia?

Well, we know of one, at least.

Located on the shores of Lake Okanagan, Summerhill Pyramid is an architectural landmark at the intersection of weird and wonderful. It nicely epitomizes the province's laidback, groovy, and unique vibe. You might wonder what that has to do with wine. Well, the winery located on the site "rests" their wines in the pyramid. They maintain that the wines cellared here have a different profile when compared to wines that rested in other locations. We visited, and the place does have a palpable calm.

Whether the pyramid imparts a quality to the wine, we can't be sure. But Summerhill Pyramid Winery is making a name. In 2010, the winery received a trophy for Best Bottle-Fermented Sparkling Wine at the International Wine & Spirit Competition in London - a first among its Canadian peers.

Sparkling Spotlight:

Matt Mavety
Proprietor & Winemaker
Blue Mountain Winery

We asked Matt, "What makes British Columbia sparkling wine so special?"

"Sparkling wine from the Okanagan Valley presents an opportunity to craft sparkling wines with great purity and precision of fruit. The naturally high acidity levels combined with the sun-enriched fruit provides a winemaker with the ability to seamlessly thread a path between new and old world styles of sparkling wine."

Chapter 14:

USA

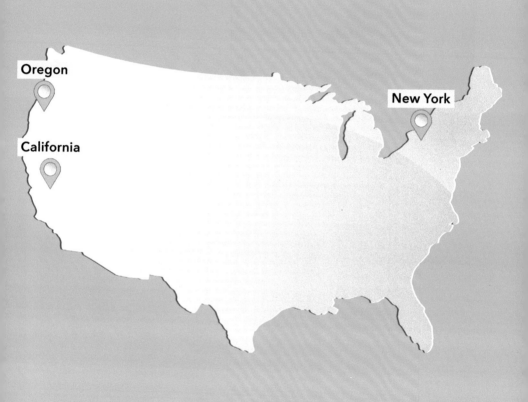

Oregon

New York

California

Sparkling in Sonoma 11/2014

Red, white & brut!

Sparkling Spotlight: USA

The United States is one of the largest wine producers in the world, and chief among American states is ... drum roll please ... California!

While known for its big, powerful reds and butter-bomb Chardonnays, California is also home to significant sparkling wine production. But this west coast powerhouse is not alone in producing American bubbles, and there is plenty of effervescent wine to be explored, and enjoyed, across the country.

Geography

When you think of American wine, what comes to mind? For us, it's California.

In the United States, an American Viticultural Area (AVA) is a designated wine region. When included on a bottle label, this guarantees that at least 85% of the grapes in the wine originated in the AVA and that the wine was made in the state indicated. Wow, that's a mouthful, eh?

There are 260 AVAs in the United States, and California is the home to 142 of them. AVAs vary in size and geography and, therefore, in focus and output. While it is not known how many AVAs produce sparkling wine, it's fair to say that some – based on location, terroir and climate – are better suited for its production. Cool-climate AVAs excel at it, naturally, and much of America's quality sparkling wine production comes from such regions.

Fizz Fact:

In the late 1970s, as California's winemaking prowess caught the attention of European winemakers and discerning consumers around the globe, producers from some of the finest sparkling wine houses began to invest in land and production in the Golden State. They weren't seeking gold, though what these early investors eventually produced did glimmer in the glass!

So, just who exactly made their way over to California?

Mumm Napa, established within the Rutherford AVA by Champagne GH Mumm in the late 1970s, produced its first vintage of Traditional Method sparkling wines in 1983. Roederer Estate, the California outpost of Champagne Louis Roederer, is in the Anderson Valley AVA and has also been producing sparkling wine since the early 1980s. Domaine Carneros, founded by Champagne Taittinger, is in Napa Valley and was established in 1987. Eileen Crane, who is often referred to as America's doyenne of sparkling wine, was the founding winemaker.

But Champagne producers were not alone in investing in California. And they weren't the first foreign producers to do it either.

Gloria Ferrer Caves & Vineyards was founded by the Ferrer family that owned Spain's largest Cava producer, Freixenet. This was the first sparkling-wine-focussed winery in Carneros and the first to plant Chardonnay and Pinot Noir for this purpose.

Production

Generally speaking, producers in AVAs have less regulatory burden when producing sparkling wine than do their counterparts around the globe. Perhaps this is the American way – a reflection of the country's entrepreneurialism and consumer awareness. For better or worse, there is a lot of variety across the United States.

The Golden State has been the dominant player in the American wine industry for several decades. It produces over 80% of American wine (equalling 242 million cases in 2021). It is home to almost 6,000 growers and over 4,000 wineries, and three out of every five bottles sold in the United States is from California.

Impressive! But what about sparkling wine? Does California dominate, too?

The data is clear, and the answer is yes. In 2020, California's sparkling production – and more specifically, its shipments to market – outnumbered the rest of the country 10 to 1. California's 300-plus producers of sparkling wine shipped just under 11 million cases of sparkling wine to U.S. markets, compared to approximately 1.5 million cases for all other states combined. That's no small achievement: foreign sparkling wine (from France, Italy, Spain and other major producing countries) accounted for just under 16 million cases in 2020.

You'll be likely to find "California Champagne" amongst that total American output. And no, that's not a typo! For historical reasons, and because of a long-standing dispute over the protected term "Champagne," some American producers are permitted to label their sparkling wines as "Champagne," provided that the brand was established before 2006 and a regional marker of origin is also included (hence, "California Champagne"). Brands created after this date are not allowed to use the term. For the most part, quality producers honour the protected term and label their sparkling wine accordingly.

But California is not a (sparkling wine) island unto itself, and other American regions are also known for their production of sparkling wine.

Just north of California, the Willamette Valley in Oregon is emerging as an effervescent hot spot. Here, almost 100 producers have taken advantage of their cool-climate sites to craft sparkling wine in various styles. These include Traditional Method sparkling wines made from Chardonnay and Pinot Noir, and decidedly crunchy and unconventional Pét-Nats that speak to the region's free spirit. Some call it the next up-and-coming sparkling wine region. We think it's already there! Oregon is anchored by top producers such as Argyle and Soter.

A little further north, and much further east, is Upstate New York – home to the Finger Lakes, Cayuga and Seneca AVAs. Like Ontario to its north, aromatic whites and cool-climate reds shine here, and chief among them is Riesling. As the Germans know, Riesling shines in Sekt, and you can definitely find your fair share of bubbly in the Finger Lakes. Dr. Konstantin Frank Winery, founded by a well-regarded viticulturist who pioneered winemaking in the Finger Lakes, is also known for revolutionizing the local sparkling wine industry. In 1985, the winery released the Finger Lakes' first-ever Traditional Method sparkling wine made from Vitis vinifera varieties. They were onto something, as sparkling wine production in the region is growing!

Profile & Characteristics

As there is so much variety between AVAs, winemaking techniques and individual wines, it's challenging to summarize the profile of American bubbles. More than 300 wineries make sparkling wine in various styles in California alone, from bone dry Brut Nature to lusciously sweet Sec. When reaching for quality sparkling wine made in the United States, you'll see familiar terms for sweetness and style, such as Blanc de Blancs, Blanc de Noirs and, of course, Rosé.

The traditional grape varieties in California sparkling wine production include Chardonnay and Pinot Noir, although the state's vintners use many other varieties as well.

Fizz Fact:

American consumers have a thirst for sparkling wine.

At the the forefront are the Californians, who consumed almost 50 million litres of sparkling wine in 2019. Not far behind these west coast bubbleheads are Illinois and New York consumers, who collectively consumed over 45 million litres of bubbly. On a per-capita basis, consumers from the Prairie State (aka Illinois) came out on top. They consumed almost two litres of sparkling wine per person in 2019.

With so many domestic consumers interested in sparkling wine, it's no surprise that so many American wineries produce bubbly.

Sparkling Spotlight:

Joy Sterling
Partner & CEO

Iron Horse Vineyards

We asked Joy, "What makes California sparkling wine so special?"

"California sparkling wines are distinguished by our exquisite fruit. The Golden State is world-renowned for growing the highest quality grapes, yielding the most delicious, distinctive, high-toned base wines. Then, meticulous, classic methodology and aging en tirage bring balance, elegance, and refinement.

"The coolest, foggiest parts of the state are best for growing the grapes for bubbly – the Central Coast, Carneros, the Russian River area (including specifically Green Valley), and Anderson Valley. In terms of our farming practices, we pride ourselves on being at the forefront of regenerative agriculture.

"The words 'California Grown' are a mark of excellence."

Sparkling Reflections: USA

A few years before we officially launched Sparkling Winos – when we were just sparkling winos – we headed out to California on our honeymoon. We drove up the iconic Pacific Coast Highway. Ending the scenic drive in San Francisco, we then visited a few wineries in Napa and Sonoma.

We barely tasted a sip of California Cabernet Sauvignon. Our wine trip focussed solely on sparkling wine, and everyone thought we were out of our minds.

But we went ahead with it and visited Domaine Carneros, J, and Iron Horse. We enjoyed each visit, but we were most impressed by the sweeping vineyard views and rustic tasting room at Iron Horse, which at the time was a couple of barrels under a barn roof. As we tasted a few of the wines, enjoying the late October sunshine in a light sweater and scarf, we looked at each other and thought: "We could live here."

We haven't quite made that leap, but we still try to find a bottle of Iron Horse to enjoy every year! – Jeff

Chapter 15:

SOUTH AFRICA

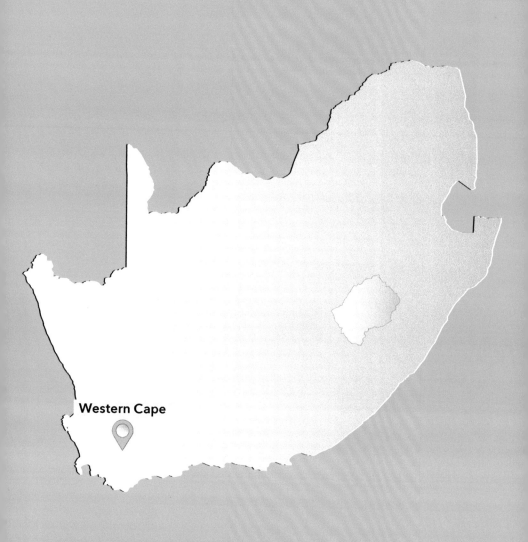

Western Cape

MCC is the MVP

Cape Point

Sparkling Spotlight: South Africa

South African wines are always a surprise, and in many ways, they over-deliver. The country's Traditional Method sparkling wines are no exception, and in our humble opinion, they stand shoulder-to-shoulder with some of the world's best bubbles.

MCC

Acronyms can be handy when it comes to wine communication: AOC, IGT, DOCG, MCC and the list goes so on.

You may be thinking: what's MCC? MCC is the short form for *Méthode Cap Classique*, the South African term for sparkling wine made in the Traditional Method.

Geography

South Africa's wine regions, often called winelands, are generally found around the Western Cape, near the coast, and are made up of diverse mountainous, sloped, and open plain areas. Aside from the Western Cape, other wine regions include the Eastern Cape, Free State, KwaZulu-Natal, Limpopo and the Northern Cape. These are further divided into Wines of Origin production sub-regions, including the well-known Stellenbosch and Robertson. Many of the Wines of Origin production areas are cool climate, making them ideal to produce MCC.

Wine has a lengthy history in South Africa, going back to the 1650s, at which time an important trading post was established, and grapes were planted at the Western Cape. Sparkling wine has a decidedly shorter history, with the first MCC – Kaapse Vonkel (Cape Sparkle) – being produced in 1971. In 2021, MCC producers celebrated an important milestone in local sparkling wine: 50 years of production!

Production

MCC denotes a Traditional Method wine, which can be made from several grape varieties, the most common being Chardonnay and Pinot Noir. Some MCC producers are also experimenting with Chenin, seen by some as South Africa's workhorse variety, and Pinotage, often referred to as its signature variety. For us, the jury on these is still out!

There are several requirements to meet MCC status, including a minimum 3 bars of pressure, a minimum of 12 months on the lees (as of 2021) and no rebottling after the second fermentation. MCCs also follow international labelling standards regarding levels of residual sugar.

The production of MCC can occur anywhere in South Africa's winelands. However, the vast majority of MCC producers are in Stellenbosch – east of Cape Town and one of the country's oldest wine regions – and Paarl. Paarl is located just to the north of Stellenbosch. Other notable areas include the cool-climate Robertson district (home to Graham Beck, South Africa's most acclaimed MCC producer).

South Africa produced just over 10 million bottles of MCC in 2020, a third of which was exported (primarily to the United Kingdom and the United States). It's also worth noting that South Africa produces a significant amount of sparkling wine outside of the MCC framework, mainly in the Charmat Method or through force carbonation.

Fizz Fact:

South Africa has eleven official languages: Sepedi, Xitsonga, Tshivenda, Sesotho, Setswana, isiZulu, isiNdebele, isiXhosa, Swati, Afrikaans and English.

Like us, you may be wondering: why was a French name selected for the country's Traditional Method sparkling wine?

As it turns out, the name Méthode Cap Classique was selected to pay homage to the French Huguenots who introduced winemaking to the Cape.

So, there you have it, mystery solved!

Sparkling Spotlight:

Pieter Ferreira
Chief Operating Officer

Graham Beck

We asked Pieter, "What makes MCC so special?"

"Cap Classique celebrated its 50th year in 2021 and we are uniquely South African. Made in the Traditional Method, whereby we do a natural second fermentation in the bottle. Only wine made in this way in South Africa, can carry the name of Cap Classique. South African Cap Classiques are the better alternative should you not want to do Champagne on the day. Our weather allows us to show the sunshine in our bubbles. The beautiful diverse geographical diversity allows for various styles coming from the Cape Winelands. Today approximately 10,500,000 bottles are produce. It remains South Africa's most vibrant wine category with the category doubling up every four years.

"Today, Graham Beck is South Africa's leading Cap Classique producer and having our Estate in Robertson we have the perfect terroir - sunshine, high incidence of natural limestone in the soil and a huge diurnal shift between day and night temperatures. This allows for low pH and great natural acidity. Graham Beck Cap Classique relies on meticulous attention to detail, dedication to authenticity, precision timing and plenty of patience. At Graham Beck our team is passionately pursuing the perfect bubble - a golden thread of excellence runs throughout the entire process and portfolio."

Profile & Characteristics

MCCs can run the gamut, but all wines must age for a minimum amount of time on the lees, and many, if not most, are made from Pinot Noir and Chardonnay. With these parameters in mind, as Traditional Method wines, MCCs will offer classic hallmarks of this production method and cuvée: richness, creaminess, complexity, minerality and plenty of citrus, tree fruit, biscuit and almond on the nose and palate. You can also expect a fine perlage.

We cannot overstate the quality-to-price ratio of MCCs. Standing shoulder to shoulder with the world's best Traditional Method sparkling wines, they typically command a price-point akin to the most affordable and approachable options (such as Prosecco and Cava). They are worth seeking out – MCC is the MVP!

Fizz Fact:

Graham Beck, one of South Africa's most acclaimed MCC producers, had the distinction of having its Non-Vintage Brut served not at one presidential inauguration, but at two!

Nelson Mandela enjoyed a glass of Graham Beck bubbly at his historic and monumental presidential inauguration in 1994 (when he was sworn in as South Africa's first Black president).

But that's not all: after hearing that Nelson Mandela enjoyed a glass of Graham Beck, Barack Obama also celebrated with some Non-Vintage Brut on the night of his U.S. presidential inauguration in 2009. We're sure he enjoyed some Californian sparkling, too.

Chapter 16:

AUSTRALIA & NEW ZEALAND

Tasmania

Marlborough

Tasmanian bubbles ... a treasure!

Sydney Opera House

Sparkling Spotlight: Australia & New Zealand

Australia and New Zealand, when thought of together, conjure up images of Santa hats in the summer heat, surfable beaches and scenic mountains. For wine lovers, it's Shiraz and Sauvignon Blanc, among other things.

While each country has a distinctive perspective and imprint on sparkling wine, they have many things in common, including their fondness for the fizzy stuff!

Geography

Australia

Sparkling wine has been made in Australia since the 1800s, and today it is big business. In 2019 the country was the fifth largest exporter of sparkling wine by value.

Wine is produced in every one of Australia's states, though production is concentrated in the south. It may be known as a warm climate winemaking region, but the land down under also has plenty of cool-climate areas (located in the southern part of the country) which offer the perfect conditions to produce sparkling.

Top among sparkling-wine-producing regions in the country is the island of Tasmania, which is putting the cool in cool climate. Located below the mainland of Australia, this small island is home to an unspoiled environment, a distinct maritime climate, and rich soils that help Chardonnay and Pinot Noir thrive. It's not a surprise then that Tasmania produces some of Australia's best sparkling wines. About 40% of this island's production is sparkling!

New Zealand

Sparkling wine production is centred in Marlborough, though you can find sparkling wines made in Gisborne, Central Otago (known for its Pinot Noir) and Hawke's Bay.

Production

In both Australia and New Zealand, Traditional Method sparkling wine can be made in any wine region and does not have a protected or bespoke term. In both countries, Charmat and force carbonated sparkling wines make up a significant proportion of domestic product and exports.

Australia

Wines here are produced with geographic indications, which can be country-wide or reflect a state, zone, region, or sub-region, if it has a definition and delineation.

Domestic consumption of Oz-produced sparkling wine is high, as the Australians love their own fizz. Despite being a much larger net exporter of wine, the overall volume of sparkling wine exports in 2020 represented only 2% of Australia's total (though this represented a not-so-insignificant 14.4 million litres).

New Zealand

Like its neighbour to the west, New Zealand also uses a geographical indication system to denote regions of wine production.

While small, New Zealand is mighty: the country is cool climate, but plentiful sun allows it to produce a surprising amount of Traditional Method sparkling wine (and no, it's not all Sauvignon Blanc). Over 100 producers are crafting sparkling wine. Despite this, exports remain relatively small overall: in 2021, sparkling wine was a distant and trailing sixth behind the ubiquitous Sauvignon Blanc and other wines, such as Pinot Noir, Pinot Gris, Rosé and Chardonnay.

Fizz Fact:

Sparkling Shiraz is often considered a uniquely Australian product. You might be thinking: sparkling red, from a warm climate region? Seriously?

Yup! Though it's made across the country, this sparkling wine style was born in the late 1800s in Victoria. While some examples are made in the Traditional Method, there is significant variation in how Sparkling Shiraz is made, resulting in various profiles and price points. It can range from bone dry to shockingly sweet, but no doubt, it looks beautiful in a flute on a hot Christmas day, on the beach, with shrimp on the barbie, in Australia. (That's barbie as in barbecue, not the doll, by the way.)

Profile & Characteristics

Significant variation exists in Australia's sparkling wine output. When it comes to cool-climate Tasmanian sparkling, much of it is made in the Traditional Method and from Chardonnay and Pinot Noir. It will offer classic hallmarks of citrus, apple and white tree fruit, biscuity and yeasty notes and creaminess and complexity on the nose and palate. Don't expect this profile from Australia's cult-classic Sparkling Shiraz!

Similarly, as New Zealand's wine regions are largely cool climate, the Traditional Method sparkling wines from this island country will tend to be high in acidity, with crisp, refreshing profiles.

In both countries, much sparkling wine is produced to be enjoyed young, though examples of aged or non-vintage wines exist and showcase excellent aging potential.

Fizz Fact:

Penfolds Grange is one of Australia's most iconic wines, made predominantly from Shiraz and considered by some to be the country's most collectable - a "first growth" wine. You're probably wondering why are the Sparkling Winos talking about Penfolds in a book about bubbles?

Well, Australia's most awarded sparkling winemaker, Ed Carr, started his career at Penfolds, sourcing grapes from cool-climate sites and setting the wheels in motion for Tasmania to become a commercially successful wine region. His later work, including at the House of Arras (the country's most awarded sparkling wine producer), has put the country on the bubbly map. With over 80 trophies and well over 200 gold medals for his wines, Ed's individual contributions have also been recognized. He was awarded Australian Winemaker of the Year twice and is the only winemaker from outside Champagne to win a Lifetime Achievement Award at the Champagne and Sparkling Wine World Championships.

Chapter 17:

OTHER
REGIONS

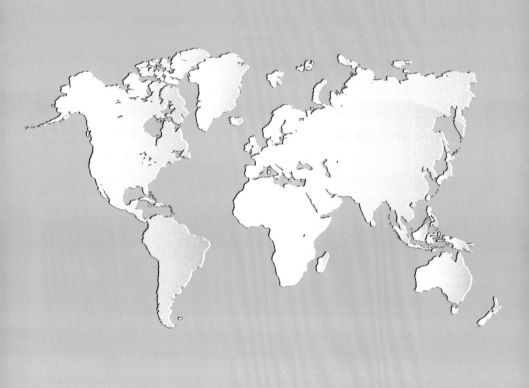

Juicy fruit!

A world of bubbles to explore

Sparkling Spotlight: Other Regions

Sparkling wine is made worldwide in a diverse array of styles. Each style expresses a local tradition or a desire to emulate a gold standard (say, Champagne). In some cases, there may be specialized terms used for sparkling wine, and in others, the pragmatic "sparkling wine" will do.

Hungary

Hungary may be known for Tokaj, but sparkling wine is also found near the sparkling shores of Lake Balaton.

The country's answer to Champagne has a direct connection to the famous French bubbly, as József Törley és Társa brought knowledge of the winemaking style from the Roederer family in Reims to the vineyards near Budapest. "Pezsgő" (pronounced "Pezz-goo") refers to Hungarian sparkling wine and derives from the Hungarian verb "pezseg," which means to sparkle or fizz. Interestingly enough, the term "pezseg" imitates the sound of sparkling wine in the glass.

Under communism, production was nationalized, and bulk wine was key. Today, producers are shaking off this period and focusing on quality. Furmint, a grape used in the production of Tokaj, features in some of Hungary's sparkling wines.

Austria

As in Germany, sparkling wine in Austria is called Sekt. It's no surprise that there is plenty of sparkling wine produced in the country, given its cooler climate, mineral-rich soils and Alpine (and exceptionally scenic) terrain.

Austrian Sekt, or Austrian Qualitätsschaumwein (Quality Sparkling Wine), can be made from over 40 approved grape varieties and must be made from wine originating in the country. Various other regulations apply thanks to Sekt having a Protected Designation of Origin (PDO) since 2015. Supplementary quality levels help consumers find their preferred style (from light and refreshing, to rich and complex).

And yes, before you ask, plenty of Austrian Sekt is made with Grüner Veltliner, thought of as Austria's signature grape.

Russia

Russian ... Champagne? Tensions between Russia and France, from whence Champagne originates, came to a head in 2021 when the former declared that only Russian-made sparkling wine could be called Champagne – or Shampanskoye – within its territory. Oy!

Russian, and later Soviet, thirst for Champagne resulted in the cultivation of a domestic wine industry that could supply sparkling wine (to the wealthy, and later, the masses). Sovetskoye Shampanskoye was created, using then-new technology, as a quick-to-produce, accessible "Champagne for the People." The generic term outlived the Soviet Union and the state-owned enterprises that made it. However, production continues in post-Soviet countries where they tend to make it sweet and from aromatic varieties such as Muscat. Most of the product is consumed domestically or exported to neighbouring countries. How much, exactly? Well, that's hard to gauge as statistics are spotty.

Portugal

Sparkling wine in Portugal is more than just the famed, lightly effervescent Vinho Verde or "Green Wine."

There's no doubt that Portugal has a warm climate. However, many of its wine regions contain cooler, higher-altitude sub-areas (including Távora-Varosa) in which indigenous varieties (such as the high-acid Baga and Touriga Nacional) and Pinot Noir and Chardonnay are used to craft Traditional Method sparkling wine. Overall, sparkling wines account for only 1% of Portugal's wine exports by value (which in 2019 totalled over €800 million).

Argentina

Argentina has a history of sparkling winemaking from the early 1900s when the first commercial products were marketed.

Though no match for Malbec and the affordable red blends that many associate with the country, sparkling wine production remains high. Many incorrectly assume California was the first market French Champagne houses eyed for expansion. It was Argentina!

Chandon Argentina began its plantings in the 1950s, seeking out cool-climate sites to grow Pinot Noir. Other producers followed suit, and the country is now home to over 130 sparkling-wine-producing wineries, which cumulatively crafted over 42,500,000 litres.

Brazil

Now, Brazil doesn't necessarily conjure up visions of sparkling wine, does it?

Brazilian wines typically come from the cooler south of the country, with over 150 wineries operating there. The Rio Grande do Sul of Brazil has a tradition of sparkling winemaking, taking the crown as the country's espumante (sparkling wine) capital.

Of note when thinking of Brazilian bubbles, the range of grapes is not restricted, so plantings are diverse and include varieties such as Muscat, Merlot and Riesling Italico. Also, while the climate in the Rio Grande do Sul and the south of Brazil is conducive for grape growing and wine production, it's not a cool-climate wine region, so the acidity tends to be less pronounced. That said, we're sure a glass of Brazilian bubbly tastes delicious while soaking up the sun on Ipanema Beach in Rio de Janeiro!

Chapter 18:

BUBBLE WRAP

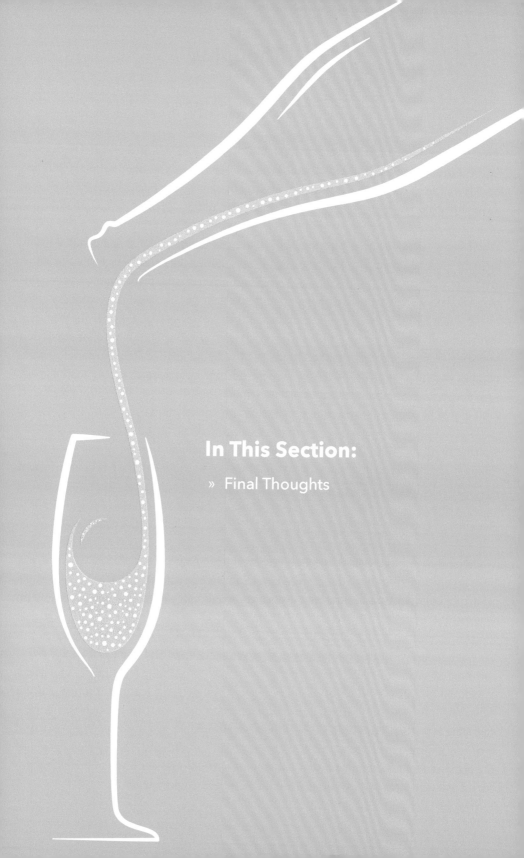

In This Section:

» Final Thoughts

Final Thoughts

Sparkling Winos started with fizz – from Champagne to Cava to Prosecco and beyond – and our fondness for effervescence was what propelled us to where we are today.

We met in 2004 and bubbles were on the table (literally and figuratively) even back then. At the time, we couldn't afford Champagne on our modest student budgets. Still, we quickly learned how to get the most (and best) bubbles for our buck: through education, travel, life experience and plenty of tasting and evaluating.

When we started our blog back in 2016, wine marketing was changing rapidly. The industry was beginning to embrace digital communication and new voices in wine. While we were not the first in this space, we think we were onto something, and soon our blog and social media channels began to complement (and occasionally compete with) one another. Blog or social debate notwithstanding, we've been told that we have a fresh, focussed and unpretentious attitude towards sparkling wine. Through a shared passion and specialization that has resulted in many titles being applied to us – sparkling wine blogger, communicator, or influencer – we have had the pleasure of spreading the good, sparkling wine word through this project and, most importantly, we have connected with (and hopefully inspired) many sparkling winos across the world.

Documenting our wine journey and dedicating a significant portion of our lives to all things sparkling has been a labour of love, and we are so excited that it has been crowned by "Life is the Bubbles."

But enough about us. This is about the most important person in the room: you!

We hope that through "Life is the Bubbles," you have found your sparkle. We hope you have an expanded appreciation for the sparkling wine spectrum under your theoretical wine tool belt (which may also be physical; we won't judge if you keep a corkscrew on your person for those wine-related emergencies).

We have given you the tools you need to decipher a sparkling wine label and a wine list. And, speaking of tools, we also taught you how to properly (and safely) undertake a Sabrage (with a sword or other blunt object). As we have learned through our life experience as Sparkling Winos – and hopefully you have learned through this book – sparkling wine can be effortless. But it sparkles brightest when served with care and attention paid to temperature, vessel of choice and in the context of the right food pairings. But remember, those food pairings – whether fool-proof classics or unconventional go-tos – are suggestions, and your palate should always be your guide.

While your palate is top of mind, let us remind you that "Life is the Bubbles" also helped inspire your inner bartender by shaking up and sharing several mind-blowing wine cocktail recipes that will take your next brunch to the next level. We have also armed you with the behind-the-scenes know-how (from climate to grapes to winemaking and production methods) and took you on an effervescent world tour of major wine regions. We hope this information serves you well, whether as talking points at the next brunch you host or as the springboard to **your incredible wine journey**. Cheers!

References

- Austrian Wine. (n.d.). Austrian Sekt. Retrieved November 8, 2021, from https://www.austrianwine.com/austrian-sekt

- Best's Wines. (n.d.). An Australian tradition: Best's sparkling shiraz. Retrieved November 7, 2021, from https://www.bestswines.com/blog/BestsSparklingShiraz

- Bugher, T. (n.d.). American Viticultural Area (AVA). Retrieved November 12, 2021, from https://www.ttb.gov/wine/american-viticultural-area-ava

- Cap Classique Producers Association. (n.d.). Overview 2021. Retrieved November 6, 2021, from http://www.capclassique.co.za/members/CCPA%20Overview%202021.pdf

- Champagne & Sparkling Wine World Championships. (n.d.). On Merret: The original English method. Retrieved November 7, 2021, from https://www.champagnesparklingwwc.co.uk/wp-content/uploads/2015/01/WFW38StevensonALaVolee-The-350th-Anniversary-of-Christopher-Merrets-paper-2012.pdf

- Champagne-Ardenne Tourisme. (2016, February 16). The cellars of Champagne in Reims. Retrieved November 13, 2021, from https://www.champagne-ardenne-tourism.co.uk/discover/weekend-town/reims/cellars-champagne-reims

- Cole, K. (2021). Sparkling Wine Anytime: The Best Bottles to Pop for Every Occasion. Abrams Image.

- Conseil Interprofessionnel des Vins d'Alsace. (n.d.). The AOC Crémant d'Alsace - Vins d'Alsace appellation. Retrieved November 13, 2021, from https://www.vinsalsace.com/en/gouts-et-couleurs/aoc/aoc-cremant-dalsace/

- Conseil Interprofessionnel du Vin de Bordeaux. (2019, November 18). The guide to Cremant de Bordeaux. Retrieved November 13, 2021, from https://www.bordeaux.com/us/Bordeaux-Magazine-US/Journal/Education/The-Ultimate-Guide-to-Cremant-de-Bordeaux

- Consorzio di tutela della denominazione di origine controllata Prosecco. (n.d.). The story | Consorzio Tutela Prosecco DOC. Retrieved November 3, 2021, from https://www.prosecco.wine/index.php/en/story

- Consorzio per la tutela del Franciacorta. (n.d.). Economic Observatory. Retrieved November 3, 2021, from https://www.franciacorta.net/en/the-consortium/economic-observatory/

- Consorzio per la tutela del Franciacorta. (n.d.). History. Retrieved November 3, 2021, from https://www.franciacorta.net/en/the-consortium/history/

- Consorzio per la tutela dell'Asti. (2021, September 6). History. Retrieved December 3, 2021, from https://www.astidocg.it/en/storia/

- Denominación de Origen Cava. (n.d.). D.O. Cava Sparkling Wine. Retrieved November 4, 2021, from https://www.cava.wine/en/

- Denominación de Origen Cava. (n.d.). Key Figures 2020. Retrieved November 4, 2021, from https://www.cava.wine/documents/258/ENG_KEY_FIGURES_2020.pdf

- Dr. Konstantin Frank Winery. (2022, March 7). Winemaking. Retrieved November 12, 2021, from https://www.drfrankwines.com/winemaking/#sparkling

- Finger Lakes Wine Alliance. (n.d.). Quick Facts and Resources. Retrieved November 12, 2021, from https://www.fingerlakeswinealliance.com/quick-facts/

- Freixenet USA. (2017, May 1). Cordon Negro brut. Retrieved November 4, 2021, from https://www.freixenetusa.com/products/cordon-negro-brut

- Fédération Nationale des producteurs et élaborateurs de Crémant. (2019, February 19). Le Crémant. Retrieved December 27, 2021, from https://cremants.com/en/le-cremant/

- Go Brazil Wines & Spirits. (2021, August 6). Brazilian wines list. Retrieved November 11, 2021, from https://www.gobrazilwines.com/wineries/

- Graham Beck. (n.d.). Brut NV. Retrieved November 6, 2021, from https://grahambeck.com/collection/brut-nv

- Hidalgo, J. (2019, December 20). The long history of Argentine sparkling wines. Retrieved November 8, 2021, from https://blog.winesofargentina.com/destacadas/the-long-history-of-argentine-sparkling-wines/
- Italian Wine Guide. (n.d.). Vinzonen Lambrusco. Retrieved November 1, 2021, from https://italianwine.guide/regions-en-gb/emilia-romagna-en-gb/lambrusco-vinene-en-gb/
- Le Bureau Interprofessionnel des Vins de Bourgogne (BIVB) . (2014, February 27). Crémant de Bourgogne. Retrieved November 13, 2021, from https://www.bourgogne-wines.com/our-wines-our-terroir/the-bourgogne-winegrowing-region-and-its-appellations/cremant-de-bourgogne,2458,9253.html
- Le Comité Interprofessionnel du vin de Champagne (CIVC). (n.d.). Champagne growers and houses. Retrieved November 13, 2021, from https://www.champagne.fr/en/comite-champagne/champagne-growers-and-houses/champagne-growers-and-houses
- Le Comité Interprofessionnel du vin de Champagne (CIVC). (n.d.). Geography of the champagne vineyards. Retrieved November 13, 2021, from https://www.champagne.fr/en/terroir-appellation/champagne-terroir/champagne-vineyards-geography
- Le Comité Interprofessionnel du vin de Champagne (CIVC). (n.d.). The Birth of a Legend. Retrieved November 13, 2021, from https://www.champagne.fr/en/terroir-appellation/champagne-vineyard-and-appellation-history/birth-of-a-legend
- Maison de la Clairette. (n.d.). Clairette de die - The AOCs. Retrieved November 13, 2021, from https://clairette-de-die.com/en/clairette-de-die/aocs/
- Meiningers Wine Business International. (n.d.). Lambrusco stages a comeback. Retrieved November 3, 2021, from https://www.wine-business-international.com/wine/styles-regions/lambrusco-stages-comeback
- New Zealand Wine. (n.d.). New Zealand sparkling wine. Retrieved November 7, 2021, from https://www.nzwine.com/en/winestyle/sparkling/
- Palmer, L. (2016). The Ultimate Guide to Champagne. Liz Palmer Media Group Inc.
- Peters, M., & Pinhey, C. (2016). The Wine Lover's Guide to Atlantic Canada. Nimbus Publishing.
- Puckette, M., & Hammack, J. (2018). Wine Folly: Magnum Edition: The Master Guide. Avery, an imprint of Penguin Random House.
- Roberts, A. M. (2020, January 17). Ridgeview crowned winemaker of Year in the international wine & spirit competition. Retrieved November 1, 2021, from https://www.ridgeview.co.uk/all/ridgeview-crowned-winemaker-of-year-iwsc-2018/
- Robinson, J. (2016). Understanding Wines: Explaining Style and Quality. Wine and Spirit Education Trust.
- Sparkling Winos. (n.d.). Two guys blogging about all things bubbly! Champagne, cava, prosecco and beyond! Retrieved November 1, 2021, from https://sparklingwinos.com/
- Statista. (2021, February 16). Worldwide: Leading 10 exporters of sparkling wine 2019. Retrieved November 7, 2021, from https://www.statista.com/statistics/420910/leading-10-exporters-of-sparkling-wine/
- Stevenson, T. (2019, June 20). Dom Pérignon: Fact & fiction. Retrieved December 27, 2021, from https://www.guildsomm.com/public_content/features/articles/b/tom_stevenson/posts/dom-perignon
- Stevenson, T., Szentkiralyi, O., & Ritchie, J. (2020). The New Sotheby's Wine Encyclopedia. National Geographic.
- Taste Hungary. (2019, June 4). Sparkling Hungary, where the Pezsgő flows. Retrieved November 8, 2021, from https://tastehungary.com/journal/hungarian-pezsgo-a-sparkling-land/
- Union des Maisons de Champagne. (n.d.). Avenue de Champagne - Epernay. Retrieved November 13, 2021, from https://maisons-champagne.com/en/houses/heritage/epernay-and-surrounding-area/article/avenue-de-champagne-epernay
- Union des Maisons de Champagne. (n.d.). Ranking by turnover. Retrieved November 13, 2021, from https://maisons-champagne.com/en/industry/economy/the-champagne-houses-and-their-grandes-marques/article/ranking-by-turnover

- United States Department of Agriculture; Foreign Agricultural Service. (2021, April 22). Russia Wine Market Overview. Retrieved November 8, 2021, from https://apps.fas.usda.gov/newgainapi/api/Report/DownloadReportByFileName?fileName=Food%20and%20Agricultural%20Import%20Regulations%20and%20Standards%20Export%20Certificate%20Report_Bucharest_Romania_12-31-2021
- VQA Ontario Wine Appellation Authority. (n.d.). VQA Ontario · Regulations · Standards. Retrieved November 23, 2021, from https://www.vqaontario.ca/Regulations/Standards
- Willamette Valley Wineries Association. (n.d.). Willamette Valley Sparkling Wine. Retrieved November 12, 2021, from https://www.willamettewines.com/about-the-valley/sparkling-wine/
- Wine & Spirit Education Trust (WSET). (2019, April 11). Sherry and Asti: Two stars of the 70's making a comeback. Retrieved December 27, 2021, from https://www.wsetglobal.com/knowledge-centre/blog/2019/november/04/sherry-and-asti-two-stars-of-the-70-s-making-a-comeback/
- Wine Australia. (n.d.). Ed Carr: putting the sparkle into Australian wine. Retrieved November 7, 2021, from https://www.australianwine.com/en-AU/our-makers/ed-carr
- Wine Australia. (n.d.). Sparkling Wine - Dazzling Diversity. Retrieved November 7, 2021, from https://www.australianwine.com/en-AU/our-wines/sparkling-wine
- Wine Country Ontario. (2020, July 2). History. Retrieved November 23, 2021, from https://winecountryontario.ca/history/
- Wine Country Ontario. (2020, June 5). Canadian wine regions. Retrieved November 23, 2022, from https://winecountryontario.ca/2019/05/02/canadian-wine-regions/
- Wine Growers Nova Scotia. (n.d.). Canada's Original Wine Region. Retrieved November 23, 2021, from https://winesofnovascotia.ca/
- Wine Institute (California). (n.d.). Sparkling wine / champagne. Retrieved November 10, 2021, from https://wineinstitute.org/our-industry/statistics/wine-fact-sheets/sparkling-wine-champagne/
- Wine-Searcher. (2021, February 9). Macabeo (viura) - white wine grape variety. Retrieved November 4, 2021, from https://www.wine-searcher.com/grape-574-macabeo-viura
- Wine-searcher. (2021, March 12). Parellada - white wine grape variety. Retrieved November 4, 2021, from https://www.wine-searcher.com/grape-1512-parellada
- Wines of British Columbia. (2021, August 3). Media Kit. Retrieved November 23, 2021, from https://winebc.com/industry/media/media-kit/
- Wines of California. (2021, March 9). Statistics. Retrieved November 9, 2021, from https://discovercaliforniawines.com/media-trade/statistics/
- Wines of Canada. (n.d.). Inniskillin Ziraldo - Wines of Canada. Retrieved November 23, 2021, from https://www.winesofcanada.com/Inniskillin-Ziraldo-TL-1975.pdf
- Wines of Germany. (2019, February 28). Germany's sparkling secret... sekt. Retrieved November 5, 2021, from http://winesofgermany.co.uk/news/germanys-sparkling-secret-sekt/
- Wines of Great Britain (WGB). (2021, May 22). Great British Classic Method. Retrieved November 7, 2021, from https://www.winegb.co.uk/trade/classic-method-trade/
- Wines of Portugal. (n.d.). Statistics. Retrieved November 8, 2021, from https://www.viniportugal.pt/Statistics
- Wines of Portugal. (n.d.). Wine styles. Retrieved November 8, 2021, from https://winesofportugal.com/en/portuguese-wines/wine-styles/
- Wines of South Africa (WOSA). (n.d.). 3 centuries of Cape wine. Retrieved November 6, 2021, from https://www.wosa.co.za/The-Industry/History/Three-Centuries-of-Cape-Wine/
- Wines of South Africa (WOSA). (n.d.). Winelands of South Africa. Retrieved November 6, 2021, from https://www.wosa.co.za/The-Industry/Winegrowing-Areas/Winelands-of-South-Africa/
- Zraly, K. (2020). Kevin Zraly's Windows on the World Complete Wine Course: Revised and updated. Sterling Publishing Co., Inc.
- Żyw Davy. (2018). 101 Champagnes and other Sparkling Wines: To Try Before You Die. Birlinn.

Index

About the Authors

Jeff Graham and Mike Matyjewicz co-founded Sparkling Winos in 2016, with the mission to break down the barriers and preconceived notions about sparkling wine, and show that bubbly doesn't have to be pretentious and reserved only for special occasions. They created the website sparklingwinos.com and social channels @sparklingwinos – and now this book – to get closer to that goal!

Beginning with a love affair for sparkling wine dating back to 2004, when the duo first met, a combined passion for the bubbles – and each other – and Sparkling Winos was born. Jeff later completed the Wine Specialist program at Toronto's George Brown College and received his WSET 3 certification. The duo amassed tens of thousands of social media followers, going on to host dozens of events and to partake in media trips across the globe. They've demonstrated the art of Sabrage in venues across Canada and supported local and international sparkling wines through both television appearances and private tastings. They also run a sparkling wine-themed accommodation for wine enthusiasts, fittingly known as "The Coupe," in Ontario wine country's Niagara-on-the-Lake. In 2019, they were awarded VQA Promoters of the Year. They have contributed to. internationally acclaimed press and they have been recognized by noted wine communicators, including Wine Folly, Katherine Cole and Jancis Robinson.

For more, visit sparklingwinos.com
For media inquiries, please contact: info@sparklingwinos.com

To all the people we've been lucky enough to share a glass of bubbly with – and to those with whom we've not yet had the chance but someday will – this book is for you.

Thank you to everyone who has supported Sparkling Winos over the years.

You've made our wildest – and bubbliest – dreams come true!

– Jeff and Mike